CASE:
Puerto Madero Waterfront

D1578772

WITHDRAWN

CASE:

Puerto Madero Waterfront

edited by Jorge F. Liernur

translated by Inés Zalduendo

PRESTEL

Harvard University

Graduate School of Design

© Prestel Verlag, Munich · Berlin · London · New York, 2007

The Harvard University Graduate School of Design is a leading center for education, information, and technical expertise on the built environment. Its Departments of Architecture, Landscape Architecture, and Urban Planning and Design offer masters' and doctoral degree programs and provide the foundation for the School's Advanced Studies and Executive Education.

Photo credits: see page 108
Front and back cover: from *Informe preliminar de las organización del plan regulador de la ciudad de Buenos Aires*, 1958–62
Frontispiece: Jessica Yin

Prestel books are available worldwide. Visit our website at www.Prestel.com or contact one of the following Prestel offices for further information.

Prestel Verlag
Königinstrasse 9, 80539 Munich
Tel. +49 (0) 89 38 17 09-0, Fax +49 (0) 89 38 17 09-35
email: sales@prestel.de

Prestel Publishing Ltd.
4 Bloomsbury Place, London WC1A 2QA
Tel. +44 (0)20 7323-5004, Fax: + 44 (0)20 7636-8004
e-mail: sales@prestel-uk.co.uk

Prestel Publishing
900 Broadway, New York, NY 10003
Tel. +1(212) 995-2720, Fax +1(212) 995-2733
e-mail: sales@prestel-usa.com

Library of Congress Catalogue Card Number is available.

Editorial direction by Christopher Wynne
Design and typography by WIGEL, Munich
Lithography by Reproline Genceller, Munich
Printed and bound by Passavia Druckservice, Passau

Printed in Germany on acid-free paper
ISBN 978-3-7913-3517-9

Contents

CASE: A Series of Case Studies in Architecture, Landscape Architecture, and Urban Design

During the second half of the twentieth century, highly specialized subdisciplines and professions emerged within architecture. The subsequent autonomy of such fields as design, theory, programming, building technology, media studies, urban sociology, and environmental studies, among others, was deemed necessary in light of the growing complexity of architecture's built, cultural, and professional terms. Within our contemporary context, however, the autonomy of these subdisciplines has become increasingly specious. The very isolation of such subdisciplinary spheres, once a virtue, has begun to limit our ability to affect change. Against this balkanization, new cultural and socioeconomic conditions are urgently demanding that architecture assert a synthetic outlook.

CASE embraces synthesis by slicing across architecture's different spheres of knowledge. It invites experts from different domains to reflect collectively on individual projects. Each book in the series focuses on a specific case study—building, landscape, and/or urban development—by compressing multiple perspectives into single, intense volumes. Accordingly, each case is selected for its multifaceted qualities and its relevance to contemporary disciplinary and professional debates.

CASE proffers an intradisciplinary platform for studying and practicing architecture. It exposes the catalytic ties between architecture's forms and procedures, and ultimately, it expands the scope of theoretical inquiry to shape a more synthetic ambition for architecture.

Executive Editor
Hashim Sarkis

Series Editors
Sarah Whiting
Ron Witte

Managing Editor
Melissa Vaughn

Assistant Editor
Timothy Hyde

Preface

Much of the history of Argentina is reflected in the story of the Buenos Aires harbor. In this sixth volume in the CASE series, we have sought to critically assess the key urban intervention that is Puerto Madero, integrating varied perspectives—both professional and ideological.

I would like to thank Peter Rowe, who as Dean of the Graduate School of Design of Harvard University made possible the publication of this book. His support gave us the opportunity to develop a detailed observation not undertaken in Buenos Aires until now.

Also at the GSD, Hashim Sarkis has been a splendid advocate of our work, as has Jorge Silvetti, and we have also enjoyed the spirited collaboration of Melissa Vaughn. Inés Zalduendo deserves our thanks for her skillful translation of all chapters from Spanish, an effort made possible by the support of the Graham Foundation for Advanced Studies in the Fine Arts.

It is the shared wish of all who contributed to this book that our analyses of an intervention of such breadth and importance as Puerto Madero promote a better understanding of the relationship between historical processes and the urban fabric. It would be a wonderful outcome of our work if the transformation of other ports benefited from the observations put forward here.

Jorge F. Liernur

Introduction

Jorge F. Liernur

Television networks reproduced images of looting, chaos, and destruction. A European newspaper called it the longest slow-motion derailment in the world. As we were preparing this book, Argentina was in the middle of the dark days of late December 2001 when, without knowing who was ruling, the country lived on the edge of anarchy. The country was in total bankruptcy. There was an external debt of more than $150 billion, an unemployment rate that affected one third of the country's inhabitants, and no social support structure. About 4 million people lived below the poverty line.

It may sound strange to begin a book on urban architecture with these references, but we cannot ignore the paradox presented by the Puerto Madero operation (to be referred to here as PMO). Even though relative stability was regained (millions are still living below the poverty line), in a country that was about to come undone at the

seams, one of the most relevant urban interventions of the last part of the twentieth century took place. This intervention is still under way and is nearing completion. The explanation for this paradox will provide meaning, substance, and character to the essays that, in diverse formulations, are presented here. Furthermore, the crisis that seems to threaten the very existence of Argentina is reflected in PMO.

To explain the paradox requires reminding ourselves that Buenos Aires is the head of a very large country, extending from 23° to 53° southern latitude (equivalent to the distance between the north of Norway and the south of Sicily). This geographic range provides extraordinary diversity in terms of weather and terrain: Argentina has one of the three richest plains in the world, considerable gas and oil reserves, and an extensive river basin. There is a population of only 35 million, and virtually no ethnic, racial, or religious conflict. It is also a strange and unpredictable country. Its low birth rate in the mid-1990s, just below that of China, was con-

Main axis, view to the south

11

sidered exemplary. It is a country that produced three Nobel Prize winners in science (and two peace prize-winners), a country where popular theatrical, literary, film, and other cultural expressions flourish. Buenos Aires has both a museum of Latin American art that receives thousands of visitors per week and tremendous malnutrition and child death rates in the poorest neighborhoods. The city boasts the glitz of Puerto Madero on the one hand, and on the other displays an urban structure that becomes submerged with each heavy rain, signifying the inability of several administrations to upgrade drainage systems.

One could say that there is no paradox, given that these phenomena—bankruptcy and the flourishing of interventions such as Puerto Madero—could well be related. Furthermore, one cannot disregard the speculation of many about the origin of funds that produced the fast materialization of Puerto Madero. However, these observations do not explain the consistency of the cultural grounding and urban quality upon which the dense set of relationships are based. Simple explanations cannot unravel the mystery of the stormy relationships between wealth and poverty, power and decay, beauty and atrocity, sophistication and barbarism, modernity and archaism that characterize Argentina at the start of the twenty-first century.

The initial elements of the paradox were already present in the early stages of the construction of Buenos Aires as a modern metropolis. It was not envisioned by its founders as a large city, but as the synthesis of a great port and a small city that would serve as the seat of government (somewhat like Washington, D. C.). By the end of the nineteenth century, most of its leaders thought Argentina had to open up to massive immigration to populate its immense territory. In contrast to what occurred in the United States, they envisioned a wave of labor destined exclusively for the countryside and its agricultural production rather than the city and its industry and administration. Part of the enormous surplus of agricultural wealth of the country was directed toward the construction of the most beautiful urban fabric of South America, rather than the creation of a strong autonomous industrial base. That urban fabric, with grand mansions, avenues, theaters, parks, and

infrastructure, gave Buenos Aires its reputation as a "European city."

During the 1990s, the federal district of the metropolitan region registered two opposing tendencies: the poorest neighborhoods increased in population, while the total population of the district continued to decrease. One explanation for this phenomenon may be the following. In spite of all the difficulties, during the last decade of the twentieth century the per capita income of the inhabitants of the federal district was not only the highest in Argentina and the rest of Latin America but among the highest in the world—comparable to the income of those living in the richest nations of the North Atlantic. Even when tax evasion levels were high, the city administration still gathered sufficient revenue to support a gigantic bureaucracy and maintain health and educational services. If sports infrastructure—especially soccer stadiums—is considered, plus parks that are free and open to the public, plus deteriorated but free health and education services, one can understand why low-income and marginalized plus deteriorated but free health and education services, citizens have preferred to live in the federal district, tripling the population of unregulated settlements in less than a decade.

Some of the middle- and high-income population chose to leave the city and settle in new areas where public as well as private spaces are not subjected to the presence and potential "danger" of the poorest. Stimulated by the modernization of vehicular access infrastructures—especially during the 1990s—new settlements of so-called closed neighborhoods or country clubs have been established at the periphery of the metropolitan area, transforming themselves into permanent residential areas, with some planned to accommodate a population of 60,000 to 240,000 inhabitants. The result of this process has been the deterioration of the sophisticated urbanity once characteristic of Buenos Aires. Many areas consolidated during the twentieth century had a median density of 600 to 1,000 inhabitants per hectare and lively commercial activity, given the presence of small stores at ground-floor level.

Jorge F. Liernur

Older urban areas are not only losing population but also face deteriorating commerce, under the dual pressure of new shopping centers and the generalized economic crisis of the country—and an increase in insecurity and violence.

In the context of an economic recession, PMO seems to be part of the same dynamic I am describing, drawing energy from a previously healthy urban center. The rapid deterioration of entire urban sectors is one of the consequences of violent change introduced by uncontrolled globalization processes. Yet some nations that seek the equitable distribution of benefits and obligations have tried to manage those changes through state intervention.

One example of the high degree of mobility is what happened in Buenos Aires with the restaurant industry. It is not true, as some analysts simplistically explain, that globalization coincides with the "McDonaldization" of the world. The growth of fast food is of course a significant aspect, but also relevant is the spread of ethnic and fusion cuisines.

In Buenos Aires the food business has experienced a transformation that has not yet been the object of serious study. There is no such thing as a great *porteño* cuisine, but in no other city of the world can you eat such exquisite meat, especially grilled. The *parrillas* or barbecue restaurants are the most typical local venues. Spanish and Italian immigrants established bars and pubs specializing in foods of their homelands. In general, however, restaurants serving "international food" have predominated. They are neutral to a certain extent, but the food is of good quality because of the agricultural production of the country.

During the last decade, however, the restaurant scene has radically changed. PMO was the spearhead of these changes, which are still taking place. At PMO, the ground-floor levels of the old renovated warehouses in most cases became restaurants, making PMO a dining center. The gastronomic boom of this area occurred at the expense of Italian restaurants in La Boca, Spanish places on Avenida de Mayo, and the local barbecues of the northern stretch of the Costanera. The pull of the gastronomic offerings of Puerto Madero was even able to diminish the centrality of the most attractive tourist area in the city, around Plaza Francia.

This boom does not appear to be able to sustain itself, however; in what seems an inevitable condition of a small market, new areas of the city follow one another in short reigning periods. In conditions of limited and rarefied development such as Argentina's, in a time of a so-called globalization, transformation processes prompt continuous self-destruction. What appeared as a solid and achieved goal in a previous stage may dissolve in the present with no plan to preserve it. The devaluation of Argentine currency that followed the crisis, however, seems for the moment to guarantee the arrival of affluent international tourists, increasing use density of the site. It would be simplistic to reduce to specific sector interests the strong attraction that PMO exerted on innumerable actors. The Puerto Madero urbanization presented itself as an action destined to consolidate the identity of the city in the face of the homogenizing processes of modernity.

In the first half of the twentieth century, the area of Catalinas Norte—public property initially assigned to port uses—was freed of such uses and became an amusement park that was still operational when in the 1960s its further transformation was imagined. The Catalinas Plan was developed by a team of qualified planners; it proposed the distribution of freestanding towers of approximately thirty stories. The authors of the plan envisioned the articulation between towers to be a plane exclusively dedicated to pedestrian movement and commercial or leisure activity. The "plane" would be elevated in relation to the main avenue that comprised one of its edges and separated the area from the existing urban grid. But at the same time, it would allow a direct link with the grid through a difference in level.

The Catalinas Plan was proposed as new model of land use, with the ultimate goal of long-run transformation of the traditional division and use of the grid and its lots. This conceptualization was in agreement with the proposals of CIAM. Another regulation promulgated parallel to the creation of Catalinas provided advantages—especially higher occupation densities—to buildings built on the combination of two or more small lots within the urban grid.

The implied challenge in this plan was adopted only in part. The number of buildings proposed was decreased

Jorge F. Liernur

and the construction of the platform discarded. As a consequence, the landscape that resulted was insipid, with no conditions of urbanity. In the preliminary stages of the construction of Catalinas, the use assigned to the new buildings seemed consistent with the national development and industrial impulse; towers were assigned to the Unión Industrial Argentina (national industrial union), Aerolíneas Argentinas (airline), and Techint Organization (steel producers), and there were plans for housing the Confederación General Económica (economics confederation). In the face of this local tendency, some architects managed to create unique solutions, but they were the exception. Soon after, and as an absolutely novel phenomenon in Buenos Aires, a Sheraton Hotel was built in the area, and in the 1970s the local headquarters of IBM was also built in Catalinas. At the same time, some of the previously mentioned enterprises failed, and the buildings that have been built since then are typical headquarters of interchangeable corporations—neutral glazed prisms equal to those found in Caracas, Houston, Shanghai, or La Défense.

In the imagination of Buenos Aires, the Catalinas area represents a type of urban progress, a dehumanized, anonymous, and internationalist modernism without any contact—physical or figurative—with the rest of the city. This form of development, which for many during the 1960s and 1970s was considered positive, was viewed differently in the decades that followed.

In the context of this late-CIAM "progressive" reading of Catalinas Norte—and the saga of global metropolitan competition—PMO came to fulfill the need not merely to recover the city's character, identity, and traditions but also to offer special qualities that could attract the siting of new corporate headquarters. With its traditions and European charm, some believe that Buenos Aires can challenge São Paulo, its main rival in the region. In contrast with Catalinas / São Paulo, Puerto Madero could offer the texture of the past, an aristocratic and exclusive quality, an aura that no scenery or makeup can reproduce. That is why the operation—as in the restructuring of central Berlin—had a profoundly reactionary character, uninformed by the latest technological means and contemporary needs.

Yet the apparent success of PMO was contagious, and it fueled the imagination of leading actors. The immediate effect was the revisiting of the potential of the Catalinas area. Furthermore, the intermediate areas between Catalinas and Puerto Madero were developed. More glass prisms were added—more headquarters of corporations, such as the telephone company Telefónica de Argentina, with a building designed by César Pelli. Enthusiasm reached its most intense expression with the promotion of a plan for the reurbanization of the railway area around the Retiro terminal, the most important railway terminal in the city, located a few hundred meters from Puerto Madero. Without any study of needs, available resources, or impact on the city, the Retiro project was supposed to extend the PMO to an area of greater value and square footage, in a delusional celebration of the ultimately ill-fated "miracle" of Argentine neoliberalism.

But beyond this contagious effect, some saw in PMO an example of a new urbanism, the result at a large scale of the collaboration between public and private actors—a new urbanism, at a local and regional level, where capital together with state entities would focus on land disconnected from its previous use. In this way, to the 1,400,000 square meters of Puerto Madero one can add the privatization of the land of Sociedad Rural (110,000 square meters), Tandanor (130,000 square meters), Santa María del Buen Ayre (350,000 square meters), the ex-Warnes shelter (150,000 square meters), and the site next to the Philips factory (150,000 square meters). Although in none of these cases did the planned development materialize, the increase in scale and complexity involved in the real estate operation of Puerto Madero prompted consideration of operations never before imagined in Buenos Aires. The case of the old Abasto market is probably the most notable example. Distinct from the homogeneous transformation promoted by urban planners of the 1960s, here were enterprises of great programmatic variety—combining commercial, entertainment, leisure, service, office, and residential uses—on land with varied environmental aspects when compared to the average urban grid.

PMO also evoked a new attitude in the city population in relation to the Rio de la Plata. The brief history of the area that I present in a later chapter describes the complex relationship of the citizens of Buenos Aires with the river / ocean that the city overlooks. As a result of water contamination, the growth of port areas, and the privatization of segments along the coast, direct access to the riverfront was blocked for most inhabitants of the city when PMO began. Beyond the urbanized area, a vast stretch of so-called Ecological Reserve must be crossed before one actually reaches the coast. PMO represented a first step toward breaking this blockade. In the universally difficult relationship of waterfront-port-city, the city recovered the initiative after decades of pulling back, which served as an important encouragement for developments that followed, such as the plan for the Retiro area. Both within the federal district and in other districts of the metropolitan region, the riverfront was a subject of urban debate during the 1990s. It underwent important transformations instigated by private initiatives or as the result of public policies.

Among the first was the creation of the country clubs and riverfront marinas, although the most crucial intervention was the revitalization of an abandoned 16-kilometer railroad line known as "Tren de la Costa." It was a private enterprise less about providing a transportation solution for this part of the city than creating a recreation and leisure corridor by placing new sports areas on landfills, reutilizing old railroad stations as shopping centers, and constructing an amusement park close to the river port of Tigre. To this development—which seems to have been a failure—other private initiatives were added, such as the construction of an island for a private neighborhood in San Isidro. Also in its planning stages is the development of an island to contain an airport for local flights, to replace the airport built during the 1940s, also on a landfill.

The most outstanding public initiatives associated with the recovery of the coastline, as set in motion by PMO, are the grand park on the river, built in Vicente Lopez next to the federal district, and the parks of the Universidad de Buenos Aires. Probably the most representative expression of the enthusiasm for integrating private business and urban transformation inspired by PMO was the proposal by Buenos Aires to host the 2002 Olympics. The plan for an "Olympic corridor" brought together a number of sports installations along the northern shore—the richest axis of the city—along with some new buildings and services, adding even more value to the area.

Most of the new enterprises and projects are situated in the north. Toward the south, traditionally the poorest area of the city, PMO had another type of influence. First, it affected—by proximity—two of its oldest and most degraded neighborhoods: San Telmo and La Boca. San Telmo, the area next to Puerto Madero, began to experience a transformation with the establishment of new computer companies. La Boca was affected by the construction of flood containment works undertaken by the city administration, which enabled the creation of a riverfront promenade. The decision there was to provide continuity with the texture of paving and urban equipment used in PMO. Yet even though leading companies related to construction have located themselves in the area, the added activity has not been sufficient to stop the neighborhood's deterioration.

In the planning offices of the city, the extension of the PMO landscape along the entire waterfront was envisioned. It would have included the edge of the federal district that follows the deteriorated north shore of the Riachuelo, a highly contaminated body of water. Beyond these cosmetic changes, the most important consequence of PMO toward the south has been the creation of a new public-private corporation following the model of Puerto Madero, in this case focused on the development of the entire southern part of the urban area.

In this volume of CASE, as in previous books in the series, researchers in diverse fields address various aspects of one significant project. Graciela Silvestri, a specialist in history and landscape culture, analyzes the way in which the Rio de la Plata coastlines were incorporated into the imagination of the city through art and literature. My own work details the history of the site and its particular significance within the general history of the city and the nation. Geographer Luis Domínguez has analyzed the transformation in use of port installations with the intent of understanding the role of the port of Buenos Aires in relation to the regional transformations that result from globalization processes. From an urban history perspective, Adrián

Silo fragments

Gorelik offers a detailed review of the processes and projects that immediately preceded PMO. He also undertakes a critical analysis of the competition results that led to the materialization of this project. Alfredo Garay, an urban planner and the main technical protagonist of PMO, puts forward the political context and economic dynamic of the constitution of the Puerto Madero Corporation. Finally, Claudia Shmidt, historian and architectural critic, presents in her essay an analysis of the main projects that have formed the physical profile of PMO, and also describes aspects of the contemporary architectural debate in Argentina.

The Theater of the Plata

Graciela Silvestri

First Images of the Plata

The Italian geographer Eugenio Turri says that human beings, when confronted with a landscape, behave in one of two ways: as actors who transform the land or as spectators who provide meaning to a narrative of which they are the protagonists. These responses construct a place as landscape. But they do not construct it once and for all.

The Río de la Plata is always there, wide and brown, just as seen by the first European explorers. It is actually the mouth of two enormous rivers—the Paraná and the Paraguay—and of their tributaries; the basin occupies almost 3 million square meters. This waterway is not only natural but historical, for it represents one of the main avenues of South American conquest.

The river flows toward the east, to the Atlantic. Once you enter it, the impression is of being in a gulf or bay rather than a river; as described by Juan José Saer, it is a river without banks. Its area exceeds 30,000 square kilometers, with a maximum width of 220 kilometers at its mouth. Traveling parallel to the banks, one can spot few geographic irregularities on the west bank that allow for orientation. The east bank is different, alternating from rocky points to white sandy beaches, with spurs of the knife-edged ridge descending abruptly into the river. Both riverbanks have been greatly transformed during the twentieth century, and there is little left of the original vegetation. The import of trees, necessary for habitation and farming, was characteristic of agricultural enterprises of the nineteenth and twentieth centuries. Among the most common, the *ombú* was brought by the Jesuits during the eighteenth century and became emblematic of the Argentine pampas. The fast-growing Australian eucalyptus was brought to both riverbanks by the mid-nineteenth century. Maritime pine

Coastal Avenue, project of J.C.N. Forestier

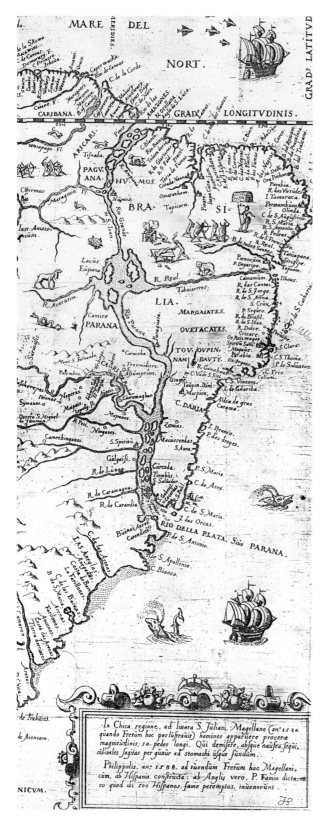

trees, which suggest a Roman landscape, have secured the sand dunes of the east coast of Montevideo since the beginning of the twentieth century.

In spite of its apparent tranquility, it is a dangerous river. Sediments carried by the Paraná are deposited, forming banks and islands. Its flow is affected by the winds (the *pampero* and the feared *sudestada*, which pushes the water toward the Argentine shore). Muddiness and floods are a constant preoccupation of those settled along the shore. In its upper stretch, the Plata narrows and gets lost in the wide Paraná delta, which covers approximately 14,000 square kilometers and is continuously growing, reaching the city of Tigre, northwest of Buenos Aires.

With these meager facts, it is difficult to imagine the area we will focus on, the site of built and imagined landscapes. But natural conditions did not affect the aesthetic sensibility of Europeans and *criollos*, or Argentines, until well into the nineteenth century. It must have been hard to believe that such wide pampas, along such a generous river, could be transformed in keeping with their dreams.

The Plata River was always distinguished in American cartography: its extraordinary dimensions placed it among the most renowned rivers. In continuity with the Paraná and the Paraguay, it marked the birth of a deep gorge in the "Patagonian land" in the area of the Pantanal, whose fantastic geography survived until late into the eighteenth century. The trip by Magellan had dispensed with any illusion that this river could be the sought-after path to the Pacific, but it did not put an end to the promise of finding the silver that gave it its name. The "gulf" area was not well known—only its approximate dimensions, the capes that defined its external boundaries, the main geographic irregularities, and the bays and mouth of tributaries for secure anchorage. For the most part, for centuries the same description is repeated, of a southern coast with a total lack of interest, in contrast to the Banda Oriental, or Uruguay, which many chroniclers found delightful.

Ulrico Schmidl, who arrived with Pedro de Mendoza's expedition, numbered the native population in the thousands. Yet when Juan de Garay arrived, the shore seemed unpopulated by people though abundant with the animals that the Spaniards had introduced, which

reproduced freely. Schmidl only briefly described the landscape characteristics. Why should he? After having navigated the Caribbean shores of the Guanabara Bay, the shore of the Plata River could not be more insipid, surpassed in monotony only by the wide muddy river itself.

To the unwelcoming landscape one can add episodes of fright that consistently appear in the chronicles of the place. According to a well-known account by Pedro Martir de Anglería, Juan Diaz de Solis, the Spaniard who discovered the river, was eaten by the natives. Another story, also well known, is about cannibalism among Spaniards. Schmidl relates how, when ravaged by hunger, men ate horses and were punished by hanging; their bodies were later eaten by their compatriots.[1]

Imagined ideas about the Plata are more common than actual geographic or cartographic descriptions. Few had seen the Plata. A late-sixteenth-century document asserted that it wasn't worth seeing.[2] But colorful notions were passed from person to person and freely illustrated. The view of Buenos Aires imagined by Jan Van Kessel in 1666 is well known. An obelisk, a classical vase, a unicorn, a tiger, and something that looks like a rhinoceros occupy tropical shores along a blue river that stretches between relatively steep banks.[3] One strange animal can be considered representative of local fauna: the armadillo. Many artists at the time show America, personified as a woman, seated on the back of this strange creature. In the Fontana dei Fiumi in Piazza Navona in Rome, the Plata is one of the rivers that symbolize the world. At the time of the Italian Baroque, the Plata was an exotic referent of natural power. But if constrained by the few facts that existed, Borromini would not have been able to associate the river with greatness.

The Emergence of the Landscape of the Plata River Region

Along with the lack of precision in navigation charts and plans,[4] there are few naturalist views of the banks of the Plata. The oldest was published in the atlas of the Dutch Vingboons, in 1660.[5] It shows an anchored war vessel; near the city there is a boat and two smaller sloops used for landings. The shore outline extends from the mouth of the Riachuelo up to el Retiro, showing the city elevated over the ravines, including the buildings of the fort and the church. Such a lack of representation will leave an important imprint on the culture of the region.

The perception of the region changed by the end of the eighteenth century, the result of diverse transformations. The banks of the Plata and its two key cities—

Buenos Aires and Montevideo—are well positioned, from both a commercial and a military-strategic point of view. The "Atlantic policy" of the Bourbon crown, reflecting a renewed interest in navigation and overseas commerce, translated into the protection of the colonies against foreign raids and a strengthening of the colonial government. The reorganization of the South American territory will end with the creation of the Viceroyalty of the Río de la Plata in 1778, with Buenos Aires as its capital. The new outlook on America indicates the new set of ideas: the contributions of economic policy, the consequent revaluation of manual labor (especially agrarian), urban civility, the growth of scientific knowledge—in sum, the themes of the Enlightenment.

It is in this context that the first systematic studies of the Plata are produced. In marking boundaries between the possessions of Spain and Portugal, the geographic tasks undertaken between 1750 and 1777 are fundamental, with the participation of the first group of professional cartographers, coastal pilots, and engineers,

many of whom remained in South America.[6] At the time, no local institution was empowered to conduct surveying, which had to be done, given the lack of landmarks on the plain, by observation of the sky. Coastal pilots such as Juan Alsina and Andrés Oyarbide are among the first professional surveyors of the Plata equipped with instruments for land measurement. Around the same time, the scientific voyage of the ships *Atrevida* and *Descubierta* was proposed, to be commanded by Captain Alejandro Malaspina "following the plans of Cook and La Pérouse."[7] The first "modern" naturalist views of the Plata banks, after the Vingboons', were based on sketches of Felipe Bauzá, who was in charge of the cartography of the expedition, engraved by another member, the artist Fernando Brambilla. Montevideo and Buenos Aires are shown foreshortened, a representation more adequate for the picturesque bay of the Uruguayan shore than for the linear one of Buenos Aires. But in such way, Brambilla was able to augment the landscape composition with anecdotes of inhabi-

Graciela Silvestri

Benito Panunzi, *Estación del ferrocarril del Retiro*, ca. 1867

Estaban Gonnet, *Estatua del general San Martin*, 1864

tants' customs—enormous carts in the views of Buenos Aires, the family with the patriarch on horseback in the Montevidean view—according to the classic lesson of de Claude. The second perspective that Brambilla produced was a panoramic marine view.

The main novelty in these engravings was the depiction of the atmospheric light. For the first time, a characteristic mentioned only briefly in the texts describing the Plata is highlighted: the overwhelming presence of the sky.[8] Félix de Azara, a prestigious naturalist and member of the Comisionados expedition, analyzed weather conditions, indicating the humidity that to this day is a regular topic of conversation in Buenos Aires. But the storms are the most feared phenomena: finally here, in the air, is the sublime greatness that the land and the river still did not denote.[9] The works of the Demarcation Commission and the Malaspina expedition are sources of detailed descriptions of the vegetable and animal life. The descriptions by Félix de Azara—*Viajes por la América meridional*, the *Apuntamientos para la Historia natural de las aves de la provincia del Paraguay y Río de la Plata*, and the *Apuntamientos* on quadrupeds—will be an important reference for travelers who followed, as would his notes on society and characteristic human types. After 1810, travelers—predominantly English—who crossed the Argentine pampas would rely on the descriptions of Azara. It is the privileged source

from which was constructed a common understanding of the landscapes of the Plata River region that is reflected in the national literature and art of the end of the century. One can see, as an example, the engravings of Emeric Essex Vidal; his album *Picturesque Illustrations of Buenos Aires and Montevideo* offers views in which green is lacking and mud is plentiful.

The Utopia of the Mississippi

During the nineteenth century, travelers connect the lived environment with categories of taste: the beautiful, the sublime, the picturesque. But if other South American environments could be easily understood using this rhetoric, the river and the pampas posed serious problems. For Darwin, for example, "The Plata looks like a noble estuary on the map. But is in truth a poor affair. A wide expanse of muddy water has neither grandeur nor beauty."[10] Darwin knew perfectly well why this river and this pampa could not be considered sublime, as there were no heights from which to observe the grand extension in a single glance.[11] Neither was it picturesque (there were no appealing irregularities, abundant vegetation, or variations in color). Less still was it beautiful, for the river wasn't blue but brown.

On the other hand, it was possible to find an analogue in the mighty Mississippi as described in the *Atala*

View of the Riachuelo, ca. 1860

Prilidiano Pueyrredón,
Costa del Rio de la Plata

of Chateaubriand, with two banks equally diverse, although with a less notable contrast: to the south, the silence of the savannah without limit; to the north, the flowery idyll.[12] After the political separation of Uruguay from the rest of the provinces of the Plata in 1825, the contrast between the banks was accentuated: in *Montevideo o la Nueva Troya* by Darwin, and in the writings of the French journalist Xavier Marmier, in which Montevideo and Buenos Aires are described in a contrasting manner. While the bay of Montevideo is depicted as a joyous amphitheater, Buenos Aires lacks picturesque character. "Beyond there is nothing but plains that are not perceived, the immense solitary pampa that continues to develop, with a sad uniformity, to the foot of the Andes."[13] In similar terms, the English Woodbine Parish expressed uneasiness because of the lack of variety, irregularities, or notable features in the landscape.[14] At the same time, scientific-naturalist precision operates against these great rhetorical gestures about the character of each place. Woodbine Hinchcliff, for example, described the band that goes from San Fernando to the Buenos Aires suburbs of San Isidro and Belgrano, the landscape of the delta, as a pastoral idyll.[15]

The writer who brings together the diverse meanings of the landscape in a clearly political context is Domingo Faustino Sarmiento in his *Facundo*, in which the environmental and aesthetic characters are situated directly in relation to the political inclinations of the people.[16] In this founding text of the Argentine national literary tradition, the landscape themes have a European literary base that has itself been constructed from art. Sarmiento, born in San Juan, had not seen Buenos Aires or the pampas or the river when he wrote his masterwork. His late knowledge of Buenos Aires brought him only disappointment.[17] As an allegorist of sophisticated politics, of modern society, Sarmiento preferred the fragmentary configuration of the picturesque given that, in his understanding, the sublime referred to tyranny, exotic backwardness, and coarse nature. The aesthetic description blended during these years with the possibilities of progress thanks to the river: his model of a future landscape was, once again, the Mississippi, which had been an Eden and was rapidly transforming itself due to technique and commerce, shaping a picturesque human landscape. He can identify it only at the mouth of the Riachuelo, the small river that flows into the Plata, the old sheltering port that he described as a Dutch painting.[18]

The technical works that followed the Organización Nacional (1853) focused on the transformation of this inhospitable and insipid environment into a colorful and

civilized scene, rustic but progressive: commercial navigation, secure ports, river beaconing, artificial canals. Toward the end of the nineteenth century, the grand sanitary infrastructure works, together with other technical transformations such as the viaduct of the Buenos Aires–Ensenada railroad, as well as the port of Buenos Aires itself, would change the profile of the Buenos Aires bank forever. This is the moment when the river was removed from the daily experience of the city.

The undifferentiated, marshy terrains of the bank had to be consolidated and covered with trees, as had been done with the British islands, although trees had never existed here. The people of Buenos Aires, or *porteños*, were conscious of the landscape value of water plus greenery, and the coastline promenade constituted a privileged project. The intent of articulating the shore with promenades had been repeated since the mid-nineteenth century. But its greatest obstacle was the Madero port, the symbol of progress. The paradox that will usher in the twentieth century is formalized: to recover the river, and to create parks at a metropolitan scale to complement the coastline promenades, it is necessary to grow over the water a kind of no-man's land. Aesthetics come into conflict with development.

The Aesthetics of Progress

The imperative of trees, greenery, the civilized promenade, and hygiene were similar on both banks, as was the will to educate the masses of immigrants in patriotic values. Argentina, at the beginning of the twentieth century, thought of itself as called to a particular destiny. Under what vision statements could the big changes of the nation be integrated into the symbolic discourse of the arts and literature?

As an example of this approach is still maintained in public schools: verses of the poet Leopoldo Lugones are often recited in school ceremonies. In his odes, Lugones recognized the need to reunite landscapes, productive transformations, and national values in a credible aesthetic perspective that can no longer be picturesque. The color of the river is central to Lugones.

In his *Odas seculares*, a georgic paean to cattle raising and agriculture, the river is not brown, green, or yellow but the "color of the lion," a metaphor that allows him to imply courage and character. He situates it with the other great rivers of the world ("and you become with the Ganges of the gods, the blue Danube of the empires ... / the noble tribe of waters that flow, facing the sun, toward the unending ocean"). At the same time, he compares the river to a track—the common motif of progress, the railroad. This aesthetic-political framing is further enhanced with reference to the glory of revolution that was born in the cities of the Plata.

Literary Metaphysics

One hundred years after the 1810 revolution, the members of the ruling elite of Buenos Aires, worried because massive immigration threatened what they considered to be the traditional features of Argentina, would change their preferences: the picturesque repertoire will be judged with distant irony, replaced by patriotic clichés recited in public schools. The will to restore colonial simplicity, the values of the "cities of the parents," the sounds of the native country, are already identified in the realm of the visual arts by the beginning of the twentieth century.

Graciela Silvestri

But it is not in the colonial repertoire where the new generation of Argentine artists and poets will find their inspiration, but in the land itself, its secrets, and in particular in that articulation between pampa and river that is so difficult to characterize in conventional terms. This cultural turn has been identified with the search for the immanent, the primary, the untouched, the virgin, that finds its material in the scientific testimonies of geology and paleontology, transforming them into ahistorical clues of Argentine identity, which seemed to change form in modernity.[19] "Each day of travel the caravels traced back a hundred years," wrote Ezequiel Martinez Estrada in his *Radiografía de la Pampa* (1933). He thus interpreted a trip in space as a voyage toward the deepness of time. The image of the pampa and of the vast Patagonian extension, their shared solitude and monotony, became more dense in the second half of the nineteenth century in a radically different sense than the traditional one: they became a breeding ground of the remote past.[20]

In this tradition, the *Geografía de Buenos Aires*, by the medical doctor and writer Florencio Escardó (1945), constructed an analogy between pampa, river, and city.[21]

It [Buenos Aires] is flanked by two immensities: the pampa and the Plata River. . . . The river carries before Buenos Aires the mud of half of South America, and it flows building banks, islands, deltas, and more pampa. . . . The emotion of the Plata River facing Buenos Aires is not a taste for any palate, nor vibration for any chord; it is about an unusual reality for which one needs to have acquired certain emotional training. . . . I have repeated an experience that never fails: during a casual walk and without previous warning, I have made people from the interior of the country and from the most different American countries suddenly face the river. Sometimes the reaction is of disdain: they find the water muddy, dirty, unexpressive; but most of the spectators remain mute and deaf when confronted with the spectacle and its meaning ... the Plata River facing Buenos Aires is an extraordinary fact of extraordinarity. Nothing can

be worse for it than the classic description of road that travels. It is not a road to leave, but a country in which to stay; it is not a current that is flowing or taking anything, it is an unmeasurable water that brings along; it is almost a river of earth, and the boats that cross it do not sail, they wander. . . . The river does not allow navigators, it requires hunters. Like the pampa.

This change of vision, from planned movement to geological immobility, from appreciation of the future picturesque in relation to the advance of civilization to sublime reinterpretation that accentuates its character not touched by progress reflects the aesthetic polemics of the years between wars. Criticizing the works of the most celebrated local visual artists, the "moderns" rejected both academic naturalism and retardataire post-impressionism. They rejected, in short, the picturesque view.

The form of serene beauty associated with the classical sublime, or with the extensive sublime in Kantian terms, is the significant destiny that awaits the landscape of the Plata throughout the second half of the twentieth century. Just as Jorge Luis Borges compared the neighborhood without attributes (the old Palermo) to the picturesque Riachuelo depicted by Benito Quinquela Martin, Gutero painted the silos of the port under the midday sun, the workers resting as if

Christiano Junior, *La Boca del Riachuelo*, ca. 1875

Coastal Avenue, project of J.C.N. Forestier

they were shepherds of the 1600s, strong and clear shapes as in a painting by Piero della Francesca.[22]

Probably the first to put forward an architectural solution that reflected this character was Jean Claude Nicolas Forestier, the French landscape architect who was a consultant for the 1925 plan of the city of Buenos Aires. For him, the plains would allow the settling of an infinite geometry, in the style of Versailles, that was no longer possible in France.[23] It is enough to look at the fragments that remain from the Costanera Sur and compare them to the wall of Costanera Norte imagined by Forestier, with its Roman references that accompany, stark and minimal, the never-changing river. In Costanera Norte there is no distraction of ornament, color, or floral multiplicity; it is an architecture without anecdote, without irregularities that, like the river itself, dominates space.

Le Corbusier, associated with the climate of ideas of Paris in the 1920s, where the recovery of classic motifs went hand in hand with the modern, was affected by the river. He was familiar with the rhetoric advanced by the literary avant-garde but not yet used in architecture. He was particularly fascinated by the native iconography—begun by Brambilla and Vidal—that González Garaño

showed him: he saw the images with fresh eyes. Le Corbusier's proposal was that of a powerful visual figuration that appealed to the senses, making use of the rhetoric of the river's essentiality as mirror of the pampa, of the *porteño* austerity that recovered the native tradition, and the unification of both themes.[24]

When Le Corbusier ignored the ravine of Buenos Aires, recreating on a concrete platform above the docks the horizontality of the pampa, when he extended the *cité des affaires* and the airport over the Plata, he acknowledged the climate of desires with which the *porteño* avant-garde had invested the river. The platform allowed him to create an artificial pampa, elevating the ground level so that the people of Buenos Aires, "the city without hope, without a sky, and without arteries," could meet with the "red sea from the Paraná mud." On a large dark paper sheet, "with a dash of yellow pastel," he drew the five skyscrapers that stood like pure geometries in the immensity of sky and water, divided by the line of light that the city signified.[25]

During the following decades, one who well understood this Corbusian synthesis was Amancio Williams. His work revealed the meaning of the river landscape: his projects for the airport, the theater, and the cross

Graciela Silvestri

were all positioned over the virgin waters of the river that did not recognize fences or political or social rationales, and thus—with more precision—embodied a presumably unaltered essence. In city planning, the conclusions were no different. *The City Facing the River* was the title of the documentary that the Estudio del Plan de Buenos Aires prepared as a critique of the existing city, to ground its proposals on those early speculations. The Bajo Belgrano project published in the *Revista de Arquitectura* with a magnificent photographic montage that portrayed, beyond the slabs in the green, the silver river and sky with foamy clouds like those of Brambilla.

Nostalgia

In 1976, the entire port area was closed to the public by the military dictatorship, purportedly for reasons of national security. The navigational limitations also played a part, and when Madero port was reopened, it was in ruins. During the 1980s, after the times of violence, the old rhetorical figures were reprised (the parallel between the river and the pampa, the absence of articulation between city and river). With the recovery of democracy, "public space" was transformed into a symbol of the new political agenda, and the catchphrase "recovery of the river" meant the recovery of public coastline space. Unfortunately for the *porteños*, democracy did not necessarily bring the opening of the river landscape. In 1996, only 15 percent of the shore of Buenos Aires was open to public access. There is a "reserve" of only 400 hectares along the city front, between the port and the river. These lots were gained from the river, following a logic of growth that derives from a long local tradition supported by a geographic fact: the early landfill process, which made the nineteenth-century naturalist Burmeister suppose that soon *porteños* would be able to walk to Montevideo.

The novelty in the case of the reserve is the revaluing of these lots as pure nature, in opposition to the traditional proposal of the artificial park. The emergence, during the military dictatorship, of the new naturalist inflection derives from the flourishing of the new environmentalism, as promulgated by multiple international non-

governmental organizations. From the end of the 1970s through the 1980s, the remnants of the political left in Argentina found consolation in this change of direction that left behind divisions of class and economic relations of production. Therefore to both promote nostalgically the preservation of industrial sites and protect the Ecological Reserve did not appear incoherent to authorities or to citizens. When, in 1985, the status of reserve was given to these lots that had been artificially constructed, natural (green, healthy, spontaneous) became

Amancio Williams, Hall for Visual Spectacle and Sound in Space, 1942–1953

a synonym for democracy, while artificial (concrete, urban, codified) stood for dictatorship.

What existed in those abandoned 400 hectares when they were designated a natural reserve? Flora and fauna specific to the Paraná River soon flourished. Although its use was later made more flexible, those who protected the reserve initially did not allow the construction of roads, sanitary facilities, or other infrastructure that would enable wider public access. They also did not permit the encroachment of real estate speculation that characterized Puerto Madero.

It is worthwhile to consider the unintended consequences of this purist environmental attitude. The obsession with maintaining the reserve in a "virgin" state did not allow a sensible transformation proposal for this part of the city to emerge in opposition to the irresponsible speculation that characterized the country during the presidencies of Carlos Menem and Fernando de la Rúa. Even less noticed, until it was too late, was that the real green reserve of the metropolis—the delta

and the southern shores—the so-called marginal jungle, was being rapidly transformed with real estate operations of a low quality, both qualitatively and environmentally. Therefore, for the person who arrives today in Buenos Aires—traveling by river as in years past and via the traditional route from Montevideo—the profile of the Buenos Aires coast does not coincide with images of a renovated industrial port or with pristine ecology, or with a modern city. The traveler tries to identify a skyline along the flat shore that passes before his eyes during the trip and is unable to see it. Then suddenly, the horizon is populated by buildings that want to be towers, but are strangely low, untidy, and flattened against the sky. "Of these empty banks," wrote Saer, "what remained with me above all was the abundance of the sky."[26]

Graciela Silvestri

Notes

1. Schmidl's narrative is part of the bestseller of the time, the American saga by De Bry. Its abundant illustrations initiate the popular image of canibalism in America. He reproduced a Greco-Roman temple with niches bearing statues equivalent to Apollo and Artemis—black and ivory—eating white limbs, while in the background a barbecue of human legs and arms is taking place.

2. Letter from the Governor of the Plata River, Diego Rodriguez de Valdes y la Vanda, to the King, referring to his arrival in Buenos Aires, MCH, 153 doc. 23.

3. Jan Van Kessel created this image as part of a series of representations of the known world. Among the views that accompany the central alegorical motif is the one of Buenos Ayres.

4. Not until the mid-eighteenth century did the Jesuit José Cardiel correctly outline the Buenos Aires shore, which nevertheless would continue to be represented as a narrow arrow pointing East, with its end in the cape of San Antonio. Carlos Enrique Pellegrini, in his *Revista del Plata* (1853–54), recounted how the pampa, the flat land without visible irregularities, was continuously compared with the "sea."

5. "Aldus Verhoont Hem de Stadt Buenos Ayres. Geleegen in Rio de la Plata," published in Franz C. von Wieder, *Monumenta Cartográfica*, The Hague, 1926, from the atlas by Vingboons. Outes reproduces it for the first time in Argentina in the newspaper *La Prensa*, in 1929.

6. Relatively few qualified professionals may be cited during the eighteenth century. In the demarcation of boundaries, Félix de Azara, Diego de Alvear, José María Cabrer, Pedro Antonio Cerviño, Martin Boneo, Pablo Zizur, and Andrés Oyarbide participated, among others. All are important names in the history of cartography, engineering, and natural sciences.

7. Alejandro Malaspina, *Viaje al rio de la Plata en el siglo 18*, Buenos Aires, La Facultad, 1938. The objectives consisted mainly of "the making of hydraulic charts for the remote regions of America and for the courses that can accurately guide the scarce expertise of commercial navigation" and "the research of the political state of America, both relative to Spain and to foreign nations."

8. Espinosa, a distinguished member of the Malaspina expedition, describes the impression of Buenos Aires as follows: "We arrived to the city by sunset, and the look and scenery represented by the atmosphere was most interesting. The sun increased its brightness with the refraction of the earth; and hidden behind the city, and a great mass of clouds and shadows, its brilliant rays contrasted with them: ten towers stood above the rest of the buildings that disappeared in the shadows. This view was visible towards the West, towards the South small vessels were anchored, and extending towards the North was a low shore with several country houses and tree groves." Malaspina, p. 303.

9. "The surest sign of rain is a band that can be seen against the horizon, on the West side, when the sun is about to set. A rather strong North wind, that sometimes causes a headache, announces rain for the following day. The same effect should be expected when at the end of the afternoon there is thunder towards the South-West, when you feel a stifling heat, and when from Buenos Aires you discover the opposite shore." Félix de Azara.

10. Charles Darwin, *The Voyage of the Beagle* (London: J. M. Dent and Sons, 1945).

11. "At sea, a person's eye being six feet above the surface of the water, his horizon is two miles and four-fifths distant. In like manner the more level the plain, the more nearly does the horizon approach within these narrow limits; and this, in my opinion, entirely destroys that grandeur which one would have imagined that a vast level plain would have possessed." Ibid.

12. Vizconde de Chateaubriand, *Atala* (Paris: Garnier, n. d.), p. 17.

13. Xavier Marmier, *Buenos Aires y Montevideo en 1850* (Buenos Aires: El Ateneo, 1948).

14. "… the church bell towers are the only ones that interrupt a level that is so even as are the waters in the opposite horizon. There is no far away background for the landscape; no mountains nor forests; a vast and prolonged plain extends, always the same, for more than 800 miles up to the Andes." Woodbine Parish, *Buenos Aires y las provincias del Rio de la Plata* (Buenos Aires: Hachette, 1958).

15. Woodbine Hinchcliff, *Viaje al Plata en 1861* (Buenos Aires: Hachette, 1955). The author was a member of the British Royal Geographical Society.

16. In *Facundo* the vast plain that comes into contact with the Plata River, and opens toward Europe through its port-city Buenos Aires, is destined for progress and democracy; while its "rival" Córdoba appears enclosed in the midst of churches and mountains. The interior pampa, the scene of unending battles with the Indians, is depicted otherwise, with the character of the sublime *terribilità*. Domingo F. Sarmiento, *Facundo: Civilización y Barbarie en las pampas argentinas*, 4th ed. (Buenos Aires: Hachette, 1874).

17. When Sarmiento arrived in the city for the first time, he is deeply disappointed. "The neighboring area of Buenos Aires is not at all picturesque, the sight gets tired of comprehending the full horizon, and the imagination sleeps …"

18. New impressions are evoked by the spectacle of hundreds of vessels in shipyards, wharves, ship captains, sailors, and hundreds of workers from many parts of the world. Domingo F. Sarmiento, *El Nacional*, 22 August 1856.

19. See David Viñas, *Literatura argentina y realidad política* (Buenos Aires: Centro Editor de América Latina, 1982 [1964]).

20. See Paul Russell Cutright, *The Great Naturalists Explore South America* (New York: Macmillan, 1940).

21. Florencio Escardó, *Geografía de Buenos Aires* (Buenos Aires: Eudeba, 1966 [1945]).

22. The polemic has been elaborated in Graciela Silvestri, "El paisaje industrial del Riachuelo, historia de una forma territorial," doctoral thesis, University of Buenos Aires, 1997.

23. Immersed in advancing the Le Nôtre heritage, Forestier may appear to us today as schematic in the deliberate uniformity of his proposals. But he captures the image that relates to the vast extension he must deal with, that of the river and the pampa; and we know that this reviving of the architecturalization of nature is the main bridge for the first modern experimentations in terms of parks.

24. See Jorge Francisco Liernur with P. Pschepiurca, *The Southern Net: Works and Projects by Le Corbusier and his Disciples in Argentina*, in process.

25. See the report of the Le Corbusier conferences organized by the Sociedad Central de Arquitectos in 1979, on the occasion of the fiftieth anniversary of his trip to Buenos Aires, in *Boletin Informativo* 107.

26. Juan José Saer, *El entenado* (Buenos Aires: Folios, 1983).

Puerto Madero: An Argentine History

Jorge F. Liernur

The Place: Entry or Rearguard of a Regional Space (1532–1890)

Before being a city, Buenos Aires emerged as a port; Don Pedro de Mendoza, the Spanish *adelantado* who gave it its name in 1536, was not authorized by his king to establish cities. After the initial settlement was abandoned for many years, the one started in 1580 by Juan de Garay was named "Trinidad," and the name "Buenos Aires" was applied only to the location where boats were anchored.[1]

With its blocks precariously arranged around the Plaza Mayor, the area's foundational grid responded to the Hispanic standard. The side adjacent to the river was occupied by the fort that controlled naval activity. A passageway to the Atlantic was needed for the silver that came from the rich mining center of Potosí. A good

part of the European supplies for the growing city (160,000 inhabitants by the end of the sixteenth century) would enter through the same place. Yet this port could not support the demands of commercial interests related to the movement of silver through Lima and the Caribbean route. Therefore during most of the period of Spanish colonial domination, the city, the port, and its adjacent territories were closed to the ocean and used like the southeastern rearguard of the coveted Andean mines.

Because of this artificial impediment, inhabitants of this far-off settlement were almost obliged to engage in illegal commerce with the numerous navigators who followed the South American Atlantic shore on their way to or from the Strait of Magellan. But under these conditions, it was not possible to officially improve port conditions. Well into the eighteenth century, and with the expansion of England—and with it the strengthening of Portugal and therefore Brazil—and the weakening of Spain, together with the decline in productivity of Potosí,

Project of Luis Huergo, 1889 (nonrealized)

33

Benito Panunzi, *La Aduana desde el rio*, ca. 1867

Benito Panunzi, *Paseo de Julio*, ca. 1867

Benito Panunzi, *Muelle*, ca. 1867

Benito Panunzi, *Paseo Colon*, ca. 1867

a new role for the area was initiated. The change resulted in the separation of the whole region that had Lima as its center and the creation of a new center of power in Buenos Aires, as head of the Viceroyalty of the Plata River. It was only then that the port acquired legal status and real significance, and when construction work for its improvement became possible.

But the Independence Revolution of 1810 interfered with the work, and the civil wars that followed used up resources that could have been put toward the project. To a certain extent, those wars were about the distribution of the significant income from customs that the Buenos Aires port collected, proportionate with the increase of European interest in the region. The ability to concentrate that income was at the base of *porteño* power, to the point that in the second half of the nineteenth century, the city and its hinterland were constituted as a state, independent of the rest of the territories that at the time were united in the Argentine Confederation.

With resources from agricultural exports (wool, leather, and meat) and from international credit, the rocky beaches of the old fort began to change into the structures of a modern port. The fort was demolished, and in its place new buildings were built: the semicircular structure for the customs office, the passengers' wharf, the post office, and the head of the railroad. The main site for the loading and unloading of goods continued to be the old port in the Riachuelo, and in 1876 its access was improved by the dredging of a canal.

Although significant, these works were part of a project supported only by the state of Buenos Aires. The conflict that kept it separate from the rest of the confederation was resolved by force in 1880. From then on, the city of Buenos Aires (with its customs income) was established as the capital of the Argentine nation and also the federal district. The territory that represented

Jorge F. Liernur

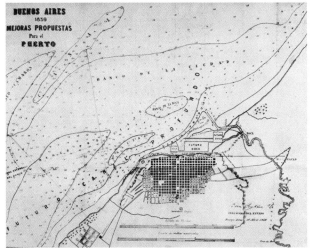

President Nicholás Avellaneda bridge, under construction, 1913

Port project of John Coghlan, 1859

Dock 3 at the beginning of the twentieth century

Project for the port of the city of Buenos Aires
(Gabriel J. Tudury, 1853)

the autonomous state became the province of Buenos Aires with the new city of La Plata as its capital. With it a new and modern port was emerging, which started to attract bigger and more modern vessels. At the same time, the Argentine Confederation had expanded other important natural ports along the Paraná River.

The cycle of wars leading to national organization ended with an agreement where, paradoxically, the forces based in the Buenos Aires territory gave up power, while the city itself was situated with greater authority as the head of the nation. To accommodate the import and export of products, the entry (and exit) of immigrants, and the inflow of credit, a new port of Buenos Aires became necessary, as a key to the future wealth of the republic.

The Madero Machinery

As with all constructions of similar magnitude, the port was finished in stages.[2,3] Its developer was Eduardo Madero, a man involved in the import-export business. Madero presented a proposal in 1869, though it was

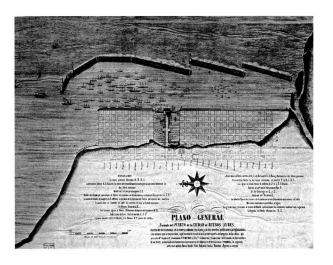

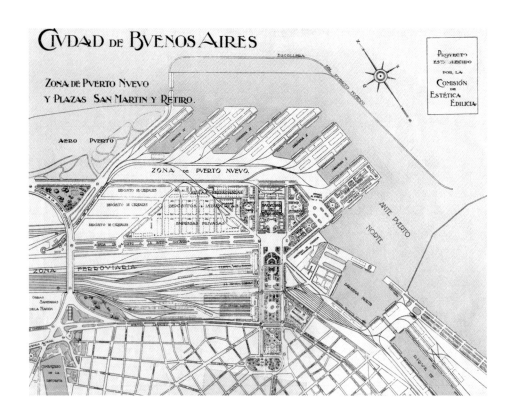

CIVDAD DE BVENOS AIRES

ZONA DE PVERTO NVEVO
Y PLAZAS SAN MARTIN Y RETIRO.

Buenos Aires, 1925,
CEE plan, Retiro area

Bird's-eye view of Buenos
Aires, 1925, CEE plan,
Retiro Park

not this proposal that guided the construction that followed, but rather a scheme developed by Juan Bateman in 1871. It consisted of the creation of a dock that, protected by embankments at each side (east and west), would connect the area of the mouth of the Riachuelo (La Boca) with the area to the north of Plaza de Mayo. It adopted a diagonal orientation in relation to the urban grid, and it would be reached by two canals, starting with the one used to enter the port from the deepest part of the river, and then forking in both directions. Madero presented his new project to the National Congress in 1882, and in 1883 the English engineering firm of Hawkshaw, Son and Hayter was put in charge of the technical proposal. This subsequently facilitated the involvement of Baring Brothers of London in financing the operation.

The president of Argentina, General Julio Roca, signed the contract with Madero on December 19, 1884, and Thomas Walker and Co. started work in July 1887. At this point the Bateman scheme had undergone some changes: the port was now located parallel to the coast, parallel to the north-south orientation of

the grid, and was subdivided in three areas: one dock to the south, another to the north, and four in the remaining central area. The diagonal line that connected La Boca with the gasometer in Retiro was built up as a protection dike. As planned for in the Bateman project, the wharves of all the docks, together with the port dikes, would be finished first, defining a sort of peninsula that left "lakes" at both sides, east and west. The one

Jorge F. Liernur

against the city would be filled in to accommodate customs warehouses and enable the sale of land to private hands. The triangle left between the docks and the dike would be used for future wharves, in case the port needed to be expanded.[4] Another characteristic of the Madero proposal was the possibility of widening the urban grid, which was immediately done and constituted an important operation for the creation of urban income.[5]

The whole port system added up to 9,700 linear meters of loading quays, and an area of water of 660,200 square meters. On the city side, twenty-one warehouses for the holding of imported goods were built; on the opposite side, three silos for cereal were constructed, to produce 566,486 square meters of storage area.[6] To connect both sides of the dikes, five rotating bridges were built, and two water controls were installed between the north and south docks. Their construction was prompted by the need to control the significant difference between the high tides of the ocean and the low tides of the river. There was also the desire to prevent the waters of the Riachuelo (contaminated by cold-storage meat plants located along its edge) from reaching the city's shore.[7] The rotating bridges were harshly criticized, and it seems that they were included based only on planned expansions. Furthermore, the export-driven uses on the east side did not need close contact with the urban grid, and the railroad accesses that did require it could be situated toward the north or south of the system. Also, both sides could be connected with transfer bridges (such as the one built a couple of years later in the Riachuelo[8]) that would not interfere with the circulation of ships.

Besides its practical uses, the Madero port was for many years also a great technical spectacle, the place where *porteños* could contemplate in awe a great scene of progress, with bold engineering responsible for an impressive display of men, steamships and trains, novel machinery, and enormous buildings.[9] The port was the great factory of the nation. Work began in 1889 on the south side with the docks and continued until 1897, when the north dock and the dredging of the corresponding canal for access were finished. The "lake" had to be landfilled, given that sewer drainage made its way

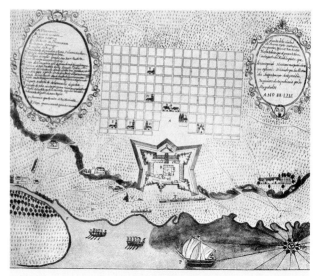

PLANO ÉPOCA COLONIAL.

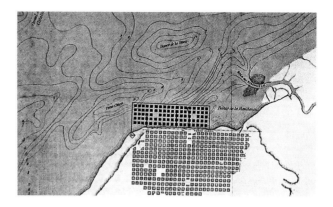

BUENOS AIRES VISTA A VUELO DE PÁJARO.

Plan of Buenos Aires, colonial era (1713)

Bird's-eye view of Buenos Aires

Project for extending the city of Buenos Aires over the Rio de la Plata (Martin B. Berraondo and company, 1875)

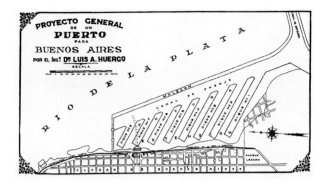

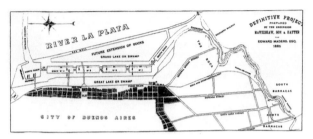

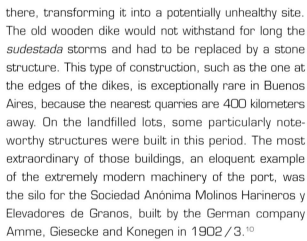

there, transforming it into a potentially unhealthy site. The old wooden dike would not withstand for long the *sudestada* storms and had to be replaced by a stone structure. This type of construction, such as the one at the edges of the dikes, is exceptionally rare in Buenos Aires, because the nearest quarries are 400 kilometers away. On the landfilled lots, some particularly noteworthy structures were built in this period. The most extraordinary of those buildings, an eloquent example of the extremely modern machinery of the port, was the silo for the Sociedad Anónima Molinos Harineros y Elevadores de Granos, built by the German company Amme, Giesecke and Konegen in 1902 / 3.[10]

As was the case with most world ports by the end of the nineteenth century, the growth of the import and export industry and the technical development of communications surpassed the capacity of the original projects.[11] The volume of goods that came in and out of Puerto Madero was almost 700,000 tons in 1882 when its developer presented his proposal to Congress. By 1897, that volume had tripled to 2,100,000 tons; by 1903 it stood at 10,000,000 tons; and by 1912 it was 19,200,000 tons. The length of ships did not increase at that speed, but the draft did. At the beginning

Port project for Buenos Aires (Luis Huergo)

Port project for Buenos Aires (Eduardo Madero)

Balneario Municipal, Costanera Sur, aerial view

Balneario Municipal under construction, 1928

Balneario Municipal

Jorge F. Liernur

of port construction, several steamboat companies preferred the recently opened port of La Plata; as the north canal of that facility reached a depth of only 21 feet, however, the port of Montevideo started to receive boats with a 32-foot draft.

The other serious inconvenience of Puerto Madero seems to have been not technical but administrative. The lack of a centralized administration and the dated loading and unloading methods delayed operations, transforming it into one of the most expensive ports in the world. After several attempts at administrative re-form and expansion projects, the Ministry of Public Works decided in 1909 to focus the growth of the port toward the north—an area known as Puerto Nuevo—with the construction of six docks in a comb-like layout that would be finished in 1928.

The existence of these new installations, and the comparative obsolescence of Puerto Madero, decreased the intensity of use of the old port. It also meant that a good portion of the landfill area remained without actual port use, adding pressure for it to play some new role for the city. Storage warehouses of various government institutions, quarantine stations, sheds, yards, and wastelands made for a bleak landscape.

Radical Changes

Changes in urban use of the port area saw a first milestone in the construction of the headquarters of the Yacht Club Argentino in 1915.[12] This event ended the debate about the location of a fuel deposit, not foreseen in the original project.[13] In 1906 a proposal had been presented for a project to widen the Madero port; a better site was imagined in a peninsula built out from the edges of the northern dock. The Yacht Club building, by Eduardo Le Monnier, is one of the high-quality architectural pieces in the area of Puerto Madero. Also in 1916, Argentina went through a decisive political change: for the first time, the president of the republic was elected by universal, secret, and mandatory ballot.[14] The winner was a leader of the Partido Radical, a progressive party with an ample base in the new urban middle class, created as a consequence of modernization and associated immigration.

Balneario Municipal under construction, 1918

Port, 1928

Puerto Madero, aerial view, 1930

The arrival of the Partido Radical in executive office was combined, in the case of Buenos Aires, with the accelerated growth of the Socialist Party.[15] In this context, social changes included the shortening of work hours, and with that came the notice of leisure time for the masses, and a new recreational venue: the water park. The Rio de la Plata beaches, to the north and south of the federal territory, would host such developments. In Puerto Madero, the new program provided a different character to the triangle created between the dikes and the coast. The south Costanera, or coastline avenue, became the articulating axis of this new popular area of the city.

The first project, commissioned by Mayor Arturo Gramajo, was developed in 1916 by the engineer Benito Carrasco.[16] The "Schematic Design for the Park and Water Recreation Area in Port Lots" spanned from Estados Unidos street to Belgrano street, and the

opening was celebrated in 1918.[17] The following year, agricultural expert Eugenio Carrasco proposed a "Project for the Port Promenade and Water Recreation Area" that would extend the park to the northern dock. Within the framework of the Proyecto Orgánico de Urbanización del Municipio (POUM), a municipal urbanization plan commissioned by Martin Noel, the mayor of Buenos Aires, and developed by the CEE (Comisión de Estética Edilicia) in 1923, it was extended to the Yacht Club site, now as part of a plan for an Avenida Costanera. The character of the place expressed in built form the radical change within Argentine society and politics. The extravagant pavilions that appeared in the new gardens reflected the unfettered celebration of the "new" by the recently arrived. The Cervecería Münich, a brewery and public house built by Andrés Kalnay in 1927, is the most representative piece of the group; many other buildings were of his authorship as well.[18]

No substantial modifications were made to the area during the following decades. In 1964, the national administration donated 50 hectares to the Boca Juniors Athletic Club for it to construct a partial landfill of an area of the river situated at the southern edge of Puerto Madero.[19] The club proposed the creation of a sort of archipelago, on which it would build an Olympic stadium for 140,000 spectators and facilities for other sports. Financing would be obtained through bonds issued by the club. The landfill was finished, but not the planned constructions or the gigantic stadium. The "sports city" didn't become much more than the small archipelago, with some pavilions of little value that were opened only sporadically. Through its canals, water circulated with difficulty, collecting dirt and debris. In 1989 the construction of housing and buildings for other uses was authorized, but no construction was undertaken. In the following years, however, some canals were landfilled, although they had been considered public space. This almost doubled the area available for new owners.

Puerto Madero under construction, two views

Jorge F. Liernur

Carretillas y desembarco en Buenos Aires en el año 1820, lithograph by Gregorio Ibarra

Horses and carts waiting for landings, ca. 1850

During the 1970s an operation that transformed the area took place: the landfill facing the southern Costanera would become the "Ecological Reserve." Several factors contributed to its materialization. First, an unusual concentration of decision-making power was in the hands of the military as a consequence of the so-called *Proceso de Reorganización Nacional* that had displaced the democratic government body. The military dictatorship had, in the person of brigadier Osvaldo Cacciatore, the perfect representative of its compulsory program of "modernization."[20] The second factor was the existence of several previous expansion plans, explained in detail below. What these plans shared was recognition of the need to provide green areas to the southeast of the city. Therefore there was a technical, historical, and cultural demand for the city to solve some of its problems by extending its area over the river. Third was the decision to dredge the canals that were the entry to the port, providing a volume of mud that could be used to fill in the new areas. A fourth factor was the existence of a great volume of solid material that would allow the construction of elongated mounds of earth to close the three successive rings that formed the landfill. This material was related to another operation advanced by Cacciatore: the construction of an infrastructure of urban highways. This operation demanded the demolition of about half a million cubic meters of the existing city, producing rubble that ended up mostly in this area.[21] Between 1977 and 1982, the new landfill became a reality.

The economic crises during the 1980s made the completion of these plans untenable. Furthermore, they were identified with the policies of the military dictatorship. The 1980s were years of nostalgia in the debate about the city and helped advance the myth that some absolute powers had taken the river from the "people." Meanwhile, in the recently formed marshes, ducks and other wildlife arrived from the Paraná and Uruguay rivers. Willows gradually mixed with species brought from the earth mounds, and a new antiurban ideology allowed the place to be constituted under a different agenda.

Imaginary Futures

The physical reality of this area of Buenos Aires is a dense accumulation of marks imprinted by those who triumphed and determined the course of Argentina's history. Projects reveal the imposition of a multitude of strategies envisioned to contrast, correct, or accelerate that course. What we now call Puerto Madero is one articulation of those varied tensions and desires. We are going to look at how the elements that constitute the area embody the images and mandates received from the past.

A beautiful sketch by Clorindo Testa expresses clearly how, within the saga of the foundational centralist scheme, the riverfront has always been a "missing" piece. A territory of artifice, always changing, Puerto Madero has performed an important function for the city: raising the question about an absence. In the imagination, that absence tends to be filled in one of two ways: understanding it as an "other" territory or as a missing piece. In the first case, that other condition may be the embodiment of the "natural," of the non-place, or of its opposite, the mask or façade that is the privilege of all coastline cities. In the second case, the place has acted as a screen or mirror on which the city has projected itself, either to correct its inequalities or to explore other possible forms of organization. We will briefly analyze these varied images.

The "Natural" Place:
The Park and the River

Although this theme is developed in another chapter, I want to highlight that the emergence of parks in Buenos Aires is tied to the consolidation of lands subject to flooding—and therefore of lower real estate value—and related to the river since colonial times. The coast of Buenos Aires long had a use related to hygiene (for bathing and clothes washing, and as a source of drinking water), while its use for contemplation officially began at the end of the eighteenth century.[22] Hygiene-related use began to diminish in tandem with the development of port uses, and with the simultaneous growth of sanitary services. At that time, the Parque de Palermo began to be used for leisure. It had emerged as part of the construction work for the palace of Brigadier Juan Manuel de Rosas, a place of marshes and grass of little value.

The growth of the city and the modernization of sanitation at the beginning of the twentieth century resulted in new programs of leisure for the population. In 1896, Adolfo Bullrich, the mayor who advanced the construction of the ring of parks around Buenos Aires as a way to counterbalance the existence of unhealthy sites, included among them the "port marshes" that we have described.[23] The park at the edge of Plaza de Mayo was part of the 1923 plan, reappearing in the

Organización del Plan Regulador de Buenos Aires (OPRBA, 1959–60), the *Esquema Director Año 2000* (EDA2000), and the *Ensanche Area Central* (EAC, 1981–82).

Opposition between "Nonplace" and Portal [24]

None of the projects previous to the Madero project (Giannini 1805; Bevans 1822–23; Coghlan 1859; Bateman 1871; Revy 1872; Huergo 1879) tried to articulate port and city. And as we have seen, many residual uses occupied the site. The place constituted the densest point in the relationship between the Argentine territory and the "world" represented by the river/sea. Le Corbusier's famous 1929 sketch featured luminous skyscrapers that were both portal and beacon.[25] Early precedents to this image are the cupolas of colonial churches and the semicircular customs house by Edward Taylor. But it will be necessary to wait until the beginning of the twentieth century to start building the idea of portal with more precision. The 1923 plan distinguishes itself here, but the skyscraper project of Ernesto Vautier for Plaza de Mayo, or even the skyscrapers built for the Oficina de Ajustes del Ferrocarril (1910), or the Pasaje Florida (1915), previously announced the idea in an incipient manner. The OPRBA project located a group of tall buildings in the northern lots of Catalinas, facing the port's passenger docks. The vision proposed by the EAC plan was more powerful, with its pairs of skyscrapers at the sides of each of the four central dikes.[26]

The Mirror of the City

Widening the city by gaining land over the river was proposed at several historic points. During the nineteenth century it was proposed in projects by Manuel Tudury (1853) and Martin Berraondo and Company (1875); this suggestion was partially picked up in the project by Madero. The projects by Benito Carrasco included the construction of an island in front of the city (for entertainment), a possibility that had also been considered—although exclusively for port uses—by the engineer James Bevans in 1822. In 1875 Guillermo Rigoni came up with a circular scheme. In 1923, the proposal by French landscape architect J. C. N. Forestier for the Comisión de Estética Edilicia created a large mirror of water enlarging dock 3 toward the river and, through the demolition of the Casa de Gobierno, incorporated the Plaza de Mayo to widen the urban grid over those lots.[27] The 1938 plan by Le Corbusier and the Argentines Jorge Ferrari Hardoy and Juan Kurchan—based on the 1929 sketches—used the port lots to provide the downtown of Buenos Aires with new leisure and sports facilities.

Both for the OPRBA in 1959[28] and EDA2000,[29] Puerto Madero was thought of as an expansion of the central area. In 1970 the Plan de Renovación Urbana Zona Sur (PRUZS) included the construction of housing and, following the "island" proposals, it created an "archipelago" of leisure and sports uses.[30] The last of these, presented during the military dictatorship (1976–83), explicitly adopted the name "Ensanche Area Central" ("Widening of the Central Area") and in a way reproduced the widening proposals of Tudury and Berraondo, an idea also developed in the project by García Espil, Leidemann, Sabatini, Soldini, and Tufaro, one of the winning proposals in the competition that led to the current plan.

In a reversal of meaning, the area was thought of as an alternative city. One alternative was the already mentioned archipelago. Within this line of thought, proposals that should be included are those by the engineer William Home Lizars (1875)[31] and of the islands / airport conceived from the mid-1920s onward—a strand that comprises the sketch by Le Corbusier, Amancio Williams's airport project of the 1940s, and more recently, the proposal by Tony Díaz and his team for the competition "20 Ideas para Buenos Aires" at the beginning of the 1980s.

Since the nineteenth century, it was thought that the 10- or 15-meter difference in level between the river and the Plaza de Mayo could be used to vertically separate the functions of representation from those of service.[32] In the 1870s studies emerged for replacing the burned-down Estación Central with new installations that would use the difference in level to separate circu-

Renovation plan for the southern zone (Bacigalupo, Guidali, Kurchan, Riopedre, 1971)

Ensanche del Area Central, model (M.R. Alvarez, R. Raña Veloso, R.H. Alvarez, S. Forster, F.H. Serra, J.O. Valera)

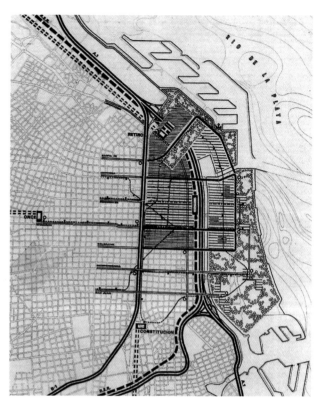

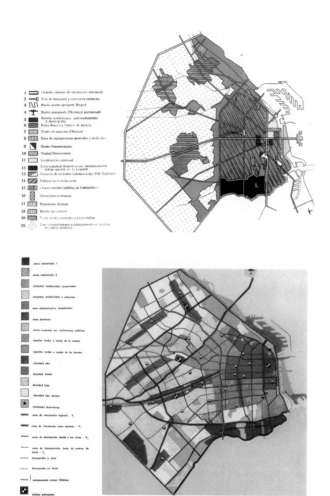

creativity expressed through the projects of La Escuelita and in the competition "20 Ideas para Buenos Aires."[36]

Balance between North and South

Buenos Aires has maintained the central role of the foundational Plaza Mayor as a result of precise balancing strategies in which the Puerto Madero area played a key part. With the modernization and growth of the city, the south expanded as a clearly industrial zone, port, and workers' suburb. At the same time, the elite moved toward the north, in part to avoid the increasingly crowded southern area.

This is one of the most important differences between the projects of Huergo and Madero: the former concentrated the heart of the port area in the Riachuelo, while the latter extended it along the coast. In the 1923 plan, the area is left as a pivot, but it tried to displace, toward the north, the industrial uses around Puerto Nuevo; and it also built along the north a gigantic coastline park accessible to the population of the south of

lation of trains, carts, and pedestrians.[33] Hardoy applied this idea to the whole northeast edge of the city. The building of the Correo Central (post office) in the area comprises a sort of imprint of these intentions, which were still alive at the beginning of the twentieth century.[34] Le Corbusier included in his proposals this vertical separation of functions, as did the original proposal for the area of Catalinas Norte.

On a different note, in the early 1940s the Austral group imagined for the area a novel program, that of "university city."[35] Puerto Madero as an "other" city had in the plans that followed its greatest expression in the Plan Urbis, given that in those of OPRBA and EDA2000 the urban grid was not defined in detail. Later, as part of the postmodernist cultural climate, the area was presented as a free board in a game of

Master plan for Buenos Aires (Le Corbusier, Juan Kurchan, and Jorge Ferrari Hardoy, 1938)

Master plan for Buenos Aires (Eduardo Sarrailh et al., 1958)

Systemization of the central area, 1962: regional metropolitan plan for the year 2000 (Juan Ballester Peña et al.)

Unloading grain

the city as well. The 1938 plan made a similar effort, highlighting the shore with the uses that went from industrial and airport in the south to university city in the north. The strength of the movement toward the north on the part of the elites influenced the establishment of the downtown in that direction and, as a consequence, the location of the tertiary office downtown of Catalinas in the OPRBA plan. It also determined the proposal of the location of new uses for the port in the EDA2000. Taking a different approach, the PRUZS tried to strengthen the establishment of a residential area accompanied by an integral transformation of San Telmo, toward the south of Plaza de Mayo. Seen in this light, the rebalancing intent of EAC is remarkable.

Notes

1. Eduardo Madero, *Historia del Puerto de Buenos Aires* (Buenos Aires, 1939).
2. See Luis Huergo, *El Puerto de Buenos Aires. Historia Técnica del Puerto de Buenos Aires. Preparada para el Congreso Internacional de Ingenieros de Saint Louis, Missouri, Estados Unidos* (October 1904); published in *Revista Técnica*, Buenos Aires, 1904.
3. About Puerto Madero, see *Inventario de Patrimonio Urbano: Puerto Madero, 1887–1992*, Buenos Aires, 1992. About the history of the port of Buenos Aires, see especially G. Silvestri, "La ciudad y el río," in J. F. Liernur and G. Silvestri, *El umbral de la metropolis* (Buenos Aires: Editorial Sudamericana, 1993). See also R. E. Longo, *Historia del Puerto de Buenos Aires* (Buenos Aires: Fernández Blanco, 1989); M. Trelles, "Historia del Puerto de Buenos Aires," *Revista de Buenos Aires* I, May 1863; G. Madero, *Historia del Puerto de Buenos Aires*, Buenos Aires, 1955.
4. That the Madero proposal create a canal toward the north of Plaza de Mayo has been interpreted in several ways. For the opposition, headed by the engineer Luis Huergo, the canal was unnecessary and its presence merely represented the intent of increasing the port budget as a part of unclear negotiations. This understanding prevailed for more than a century, until a new political understanding was put forward by the historian James Scobie, who suggested the idea of a "northern political party"—

cosmopolitan and related to large international economic interests—that would have been behind Madero's proposal, aligned against a "southern political party" of nationalist origin and associated with the traditional *porteño* power, which supported Huergo's proposal. James Scobie, *Buenos Aires del Centro a los Barrios, 1870–1910* (Buenos Aires: Ediciones Solar, 1986). Graciela Silvestri has demonstrated that the division described by Scobie does not do justice to the political reality of Argentina, however, where interests and characters were intertwined in a much more complex manner than the simple scheme presented by Scobie. On the other hand, it is evident that the North dock, where the careening dikes gave way to the only perpendicular wharfs to the shore, allowed for the creation of a port area with greater relation to the railroad lines, which came mainly from the north. This zone was nonexistent in Huergo's proposal.
5. "The future of real estate for our capital is in the port lots. It is quite clear from the few buildings that exist there, and that already today provide greater income than those located in the best neighborhoods of the city." "Los terrenos del Puerto," *La Nación* 5, 1897.
6. The data is from *The Argentine Year Book, 1903* (Buenos Aires: South American Publishing Company, 1903).
7. See Silvestri, this volume.
8. It is possible that the whole enterprise was exaggerated to obtain greater earnings. But it is difficult to understand that maximum port efficiency would not be sought, given its vital interest for

both importers and exporters who supported its construction. As has been pointed out by Silvestri, the problem seems to have resided in excessive trust in technical solutions, a trust not always justified.

9. The opening is described in *La Nación* as a popular extravaganza, with an attendance of about 60,000 people. The ceremony presented an opportunity for technological exhibitionism: the authorities arrived by train, were then taken in a steamboat, and later visited the hydraulic machinery and workshops.

10. Given its organization, mechanisms, and construction intelligence, the huge building represented one of the most advanced examples of worldwide engineering. It would become one of the favorite references of the founders of international architectural modernism. See F. Grementieri, "La presencia de la cultura arquitectónica alemana en la Argentina — valoración y preservación de testimonios tangibles," lecture presented to the international symposium Coloquio Internacional "Tras las huellas de los arquitectos alemanes en América Latina," Instituto Iberoamericano / GALA, Berlin, 2001. Walter Gropius included the project in his article "Die Entwicklung moderner Industriebaukunst," in *Jahrbuch des Deutschen Werkbund* in 1913, but it is possible that he became interested in the topic five years before, when he had to build for his family a silo in Gut Janikow (see Reginald R. Issacs, *Walter Gropius, der Mensch und sein Werk*, Berlin, 1983). At the time, the Buenos Aires silo had recently been published in *Der Industriebau*. Le Corbusier did the same in *Vers une Architecture*, and among the many texts that reproduce this example is Wilhelm Worringen's *Egyptian Art*.

11. In 1922, in the *Enciclopedia Universal Europeo-Americana*, the entry for "port" would read: "Except on rare occasions, the great ports have been built not as the result of complete plans, but have been enlarged as neded according to demands, and therefore it is not rare to find in them something technically open to critique."

12. Yacht Club Argentino, *La historia de los primeros 100 años, 1883–1993* (Buenos Aires, 1993).

13. The fuels were coal, kerosene, and mineral oils (petroleum). If the use of the first is related to steam power and the British influence in Argentina (by the beginning of the twentieth century, 1,200,000 tons of coal came from British sources), the last is associated with the period of combustion engines and the growth of influence of the United States in the region. The decision to site the flammables in the south reinforced its industrial character.

14. Participation in previous elections was restricted to "qualified" citizens.

15. In the 1913 National Congress elections, the Socialist Party obtained 50,000 votes against 32,000 obtained by the *radicales*, a difference also expressed in the composition of the City Council, where the socialists would advance to reach the majority in 1920.

16. The idea was to build a swimming pool using spring water, supposedly from a source at the site, and of a promenade along which to enjoy the gardens and river breeze. The materialization was less grand than that initial idea, and the installations were later referred to by Carrasco as "modest and minimal." See S. Berjman, ed., *Benito Carrasco, sus textos* (Buenos Aires: Facultad de Agronomía, 1997).

17. B. Carrasco, "La Avenida de la Costa," *La Nación*, February 11, 1924, and "El Balneario Municipal," *La Nación*, December 27, 1925, in Berjman.

18. About this project, see A. Kalnay, "Cervecería Munich," in *CACYA* 9, February 1928, pp. 191–208, and E. Kalnay, "La costanera sur," in *Consejo Profesional de Arquitctura y Urbanismo* 2 / 1989, pp. 6–7.

19. *Actas de Sesiones de la Honorable Cámara de Diputados de la Nación*, October 1964.

20. For the modernization role of the military dictatorship in the city of Buenos Aires, see A. Gorelik and G. Silvestri, "Ciudad y Cultura Urbana, 1976–1999: el fin de la expansión," in L. A. Romero, *Buenos Aires*.

21. I was a junior urban designer of the EAC team and thus can provide personal testimony of the facts described here.

22. The first public space planted with trees to enhance its use for recreation was located along the shore of the La Alameda river; this idea was envisioned by the Viceroy Francisco de Paula Bucarelli in 1776 and acted on later by the Viceroy Juan José Vértiz, as part of a plan to build a promenade to the river from the Plaza.

23. "The Maldonado stream, the wetlands of Flores, the Mataderos, the Riachuelo, La Boca, and the lakes of the port surround it (the city) like a chain whose links are marshes, lakes, puddles of stagnant waters, and deposits of garbage, reinforced by a rosary of factories, workshops and other industrial establishments." *Revista Municipal* III, 1896 (quoted in Scobie). The parks project of the Rio de la Plata riverside up to the mouth of the delta was put forward by Carrasco; the municipal water park was a segment of it.

24. I have developed the topic of the central area as a portal in "Area Central Norte: Reflexiones para una crítica," in *SUMMA*, February / March 1982, and in "Rascacielos de Buenos Aires," *Nuestra Arquitectura*, Buenos Aires, July 1980.

25. About the Le Corbusier proposal for Buenos Aires, see J. F. Liernur (with P. Pschepiurca), *The Southern Net: Works and Projects by Le Corbusier and his Disciples in Argentina*, in process.

26. This image of portal has been powerful, that it has survived the changes in structure of the Buenos Aires territory. During the twentieth century, the situation of Puerto Madero as entry portal to the city has changed—not only because the area lost importance in relation to the installations of Puerto Nuevo and Costanera Norte, but also (and especially from the 1940s onward), the city built a new entry, the Ezeiza International Airport, and with it invigorated the southwest as its new, and totally different, façade. The idea of the southwest of the city as a new façade has been developed by A. Ballent, "Las huellas de la política. Arquitectura, vivienda y ciudad en las propuestas del peronismo. Buenos Aires, 1946–1955," Buenos Aires, 2005.

27. J. A. Briano, "Transformaciones de nuestro Puerto en el Gran Puerto de Buenos Aires. Coordinacion Ferroviaria y Ubicación Definitiva de los Elevadores de Granos en el Mismo," in *La Ingeniería*, 681, Buenos Aires, 1931.

28. Municipalidad de Buenos Aires, Organización del Plan Regulador, *Plan Regulador: Distribución espacial de la población y usos del suelo*, Buenos Aires, 1968.

29. J. A. Ballester Peña, director, *Esquema Director Año 2000*, Secretaría del Consejo Nacional de Desarrollo—Oficina Regional de Desarrollo Area Metropolitana, Buenos Aires, 1969–70

30. J. Kurchan, J. Bacigalupo, and D. Batalla, D., *Plan de Renovación Urbana de la Zona Sur de la Ciudad de Buenos Aires*, Municipalidad de la Ciudad de Buenos Aires, Buenos Aires, 1970.

Jorge F. Liernur

31. See Harris and Company, *Proyecto para la construcción de diques flotantes, secos y de marea y otras comodidades para el puerto de Buenos Aires, presentado al Gobierno Nacional por el Ingeniero William Home Lizars*, Buenos Aires, 1875.

32. It proposed the widening of the city over the area, building the new area over hollow vaults and using it for vehicular circulation, storage, and other infrastructure.

33. It is not surprising that, in the same fashion, the initial sketches of Madero himself also proposed leaving the lower levels of dikes as voids or hollow for similar purposes.

34. Its access level would be located at the level of the Plaza, allowing it to connect to the city with bridges, leaving a service level at the lower level directly linked with the old Paseo de Julio. See Liernur, *Area Central Norte*.

35. The proposal included not only classroom buildings but also hospitals, housing, museums, labs, auditoriums, and sports centers, comprising a true alternative and autonomous urban organization. See Liernur, *The Southern Net*.

36. See C. Blazica and L. Spinadel, eds., "20 Ideas para Buenos Aires," in *Summarios* 119 and 120, Buenos Aires, 1987.

Immigrants disembarking from boat, ca. 1930

Urban Reconversion and Port Uses

Luis Javier Domínguez Roca

The renovation and adaptive reuse of Puerto Madero is one more case in a worldwide move toward the transformation of ports, which includes the renovation of obsolete port areas for new uses, the modernization of active areas, and the creation of completely new ports.[1] These trends reflect a number of factors: globalization of trade, technological transformations in maritime transportation, increase in competition both between ports and between cities, processes of regional integration, deregulation and privatization of economic activities, decentralization of functions previously exercised by nation-states, changes in urban policies, and transformations in cultural and consumer norms. This essay considers the renovation of Puerto Madero in relation to its regional, national, and local context, with particular reference to the port restructuring processes.

Bridge of the Woman, Santiago Calatrava

Current Role of the Buenos Aires Port

Buenos Aires was for many years the main port in Argentina, for both the export of agricultural goods and the import of goods and manufactured articles. It later lost its relevance as an export center, replaced by other ports such as Rosario, Bahía Blanca, and Quequén for the export of cereals and by the ports between Rosario and Santa Fe for the export of soybeans and their byproducts, among other goods.

It is still the main port, however, for imports, and it almost has a monopoly over the movement of containers. The group formed by the port of Buenos Aires and the neighboring port of Dock Sud (which until 1993 was a part of the former) concentrated 96 percent of the total movement of containers in the country in 1999.[2]

Comparing tables 1 and 2, one can see that Buenos Aires's near monopoly over the movement of containers in Argentina is not repeated for other countries in

Rank	Port*	Country	1998	1999	Var.%
1	Colon (a)	Panama	1,117,035	1,175,673	5.2
2	Buenos Aires (b)	Argentina	1,139,730	1,076,102	-5.6
3	Santos (c)	Brazil	799,476	866,811	8.4
4	Port Limon-Moin	Costa Rica	452,076	590,259	30.6
5	Port Cabello	Venezuela	486,824	496,315	1.9
6	Callao	Peru	378,013	385,820	2.1
7	Guayaquil	Ecuador	407,434	380,470	-6.6
8	San Antonio	Chile	415,001	374,945	-9.7
9	Cartagena	Colombia	277,686	281,568	1.4
10	Valparaiso	Chile	255,687	278,142	8.8
11	Port Cortes	Honduras	362,064	273,336	-24.5
12	Rio Grande	Brazil	223,133	261,660	17.3
13	Buenaventura	Colombia	247,653	250,299	1.1
14	Montevideo	Uruguay	265,892	250,227	-5.9
15	La Guaira	Venezuela	302,333	237,782	-21.4
16	Santo Tomas de Castilla	Guatemala	145,295	211,173	45.3
17	Rio de Janeiro	Brazil	195,616	205.935	5.3

* Ports included are only those that during 1999 moved more than 200,000 TEUs.
(a): Includes MIT, Evergreen, Panama Port.
(b): Includes Exolgán (Dock Sud).
(c): Includes Cosipa.
Sources: Produced by the author based on data published by *Anuario Portuario y Marítimo*, 2000; *El Observador*, 3/13/2001; CEPAL.

Table 1: Ports of Central and South America. Container movement, 1998 and 1999 (in TEUs)

Country*	1997	1998	1999	Var. % 98/97	Var. % 99/98
Brazil	1,926.171	2,009,096	1,988,830	4.3	-1.0
Panama	653,579	1,166,357	1,175,674	78.5	0.8
Argentina	1,039,575	1,174,694	1,119,824	13.0	-4.7
Chile	1,026,805	1,075,064	1,102,092	4.7	2.5

* Countries included are only those with ports that moved more than 1,000,000 TEUs in 1999. Sources: *Anuario Portuario y Marítimo* 2000; *El Observador*, 3/13/2001; CEPAL.

Table 2: Ports of Central and South America. Container movement, grouped by country (1997, 1998, 1999, in TEUs)

the region. In Brazil, the three main ports (Santos, Rio Grande, and Rio de Janeiro) move a total of 1,334,406 TEUs, representing 67.1 percent of the national total; if the ports of Paranaguá and Itajaí are added, the proportion increases to 75 percent. In Chile, the ports of San Antonio and Valparaíso move 653,087 TEUs (59.2 percent of the total). In this case, the figures show at the same time a tendency toward a greater dispersal both by the decrease of the difference between San Antonio and Valparaíso and by the increase of participation by other minor ports.

The quasi monopoly of Buenos Aires and Dock Sud could well change in the near future. Ports such as Zárate, Rosario, and La Plata are preparing to compete in the movement of containers. In Zárate, located 111 km north of Buenos Aires on the Paraná river, a private consortium has opened a terminal that could move up to 100,000 TEUs in a first phase. In Rosario a multiuse terminal has been concessioned, and in La Plata a master plan that could include a container terminal is being developed. At the same time, Uruguayan and Brazilian ports compete for a part of the current movement in Buenos Aires. The snapshot of the port's condition presented in tables 1 and 2 in comparison with that of other Latin American ports represents only a moment in what is actually a dynamic process. The relative position of each port has shifted and will continue to shift as the result of multiple factors, including deregulation and privatization, as well as the economic evolution of the various countries.

Port-Port Reconversion: Privatization and Modernization

The process of port modernization started in Argentina in 1992 with a presidential decree that deregulated maritime, river, and port activity, opening the services of pilotage, towing, and stowing. That same year the new Ley de Puertos allowed the transfer of administration of ports to their corresponding provinces. The law also provided for the transfer of the Buenos Aires port to the municipality of the city of Buenos Aires, but this was later vetoed by another presidential decree. The law established that for the larger ports, administration would be in the hands of "autonomous entities" or "administrative corporations," with representatives of the various interested parties. The situation of private port terminals that existed in several areas of the country was normalized.

In 1994 the process of privatization of the working areas of the port of Buenos Aires was initiated, guided by the national government. Most of the Puerto Nuevo area had already been separated from port activity beginning in 1989. The Dock Sud area was transferred to the government of the province of Buenos Aires,

Luis Javier Domínguez Roca

View toward the east

which authorized the construction of a container terminal by a private consortium. The Puerto Nuevo area remained in the hands of the national government and was divided into six terminals that were handed over to private operators by concession.

Port-City Reconversion: Puerto Madero, Pioneering Operation

The renovation and adaptive reuse of Puerto Madero is the first operation of its kind in Latin America. To this day there are no other projects comparable in scale, developed around a single port element. The "waterfront" reconversion projects being developed in other Latin American cities are smaller or developed from a multiplicity of elements previously assigned to different uses. Worth highlighting, however, are two projects being developed in Brazil and Uruguay. They are the revitalization of the maritime area of Rio de Janeiro,[3] and the revitalization of the La Aguada neighborhood in Montevideo (Plan Fénix).[4]

The development of Puerto Madero predates these projects. It begins in November 1989 with the creation of the Corporación Antiguo Puerto Madero (CAPM). This organization is a public limited corporation, with the nation-state and the city of Buenos Aires as its owners, in equal parts. Its purpose is the reconversion of 170 hectares of the old port for urban use.

Elsewhere in this book the characteristics and results of this process are explained. Here I will concentrate in the analysis of this operation in its global, regional, and local contexts. What specific factors have made Puerto Madero a pioneering case at the regional scale? Which elements enabled this process to begin several years before other interventions in obsolete port areas of other cities of the so-called southern cone (Argentina, Brazil, Chile, Uruguay)?

We can point to the following:

1. The object (area) of the reconversion: the existence of an extensive obsolete port area next to the central area of one of the major metropolises of Latin America.

2. The national context: a process of capitalist neoliberal restructuring of the state and society

as of 1989, with an accelerated pace compared to other countries of the region, except Chile.

3. The actors of the reconversion: a) a convergence of interests among national and local governments and the private sector; b) the presence of a group of urbanists, knowledgeable about recent trends within the discipline, particularly concerning the cases of London and Barcelona.

Port-City Reconversion and Port-Port Reconversion: The Relationship between Puerto Madero and Puerto Nuevo

The Reconversion of Puerto Nuevo

Since the concession of Puerto Nuevo to private hands, there has been a deep transformation in the operating conditions of the port.[5] Private companies made impor-

Northern side, old cranes

tant investments in capital and technology, increasing the intensity of use of port land; there was a reduction in the labor force used and an upgrade in its composition; and there was a reduction of costs and an increase in the efficiency of port operations. Figures for 1991 and 1995 show the magnitude and speed of these transformations: in that period, augmentations in equipment allowed included an increase from three to thirteen container cranes in operation; the median stay per container ship was reduced from 2.5 to 1.5 days; the import cost of a container was lowered from U.S. $450 to $120; and productivity was increased from 800 to 3,000 tons / person / year. The greater efficiency and decrease in cost translated into a significant increase in the movement of cargo. The volume for general cargo increased from 4 million tons in 1991 to 6 million tons in 1995. Container movement increased from 272,608 to 504,630 TEUs in the same period. If to the latter figure we add the 133,643 TEUs of Dock Sud (that in 1991 was still a part of the Buenos Aires port), the total for 1995 grows to 638,273 TEUs.[6] At the same time, the incorporation of technology considerably reduced the personnel used in the port. The number of workers in charge of stowing who belonged to the Administración General de Puertos was reduced from 3,200 to 1,200, and administrative employees from 3,980 to 630.[7] Union labor agreements for port operators were no longer in effect.

The growth of port activity continued until 1998. That year, the movement of containers in Buenos Aires and Dock Sud added up to approximately 1,200,000 TEUs, of which over 800,000 were from the Puerto Nuevo terminals (see table 3). From then on, the Argentine economy fell into a deep recession. The crisis generated a 9 percent reduction in the movement of containers during 1999. This relapse was more acute in Puerto Madero (11 percent) than in Dock Sud (3.4 percent). During 2000, there was a small recovery, although activity never reached 1998 levels. Given the

Luis Javier Domínguez Roca

difficulties created by the recession, reduction in total movement, and the increase in competition among terminals, operators began to develop strategies that in some cases implied mergers or acquisition of terminals by other operators. As a consequence, the consortiums in charge of the terminals have undertaken important transformations, including the reduction of terminals in Puerto Nuevo from six to three.

One issue still awaiting resolution is the delayed transfer of the port to the administration of the city of Buenos Aires. The Buenos Aires port is the only one that has continued to remain in the hands of the federal state, through the Administración General de Puertos. The main argument to justify this situation was the particular legal status of the federal district, where the mayor was once designated by the president of the country and not voted for by the local population. The reform of the National Constitution, sanctioned in 1994, declared the autonomy of the city of Buenos Aires. In 1996 its own constitution was promulgated, and the citizens of Buenos Aires voted for the first time for the leader of their city. The city constitution establishes that the port is part of its public domain. However, the national government has not yet put this transfer into effect. Nor has the structure of the administrative body of the port (Sociedad Administradora del Puerto) been defined. This body is an autonomous entity that will include representatives of the various parties involved in port operations.

Year	Puerto Nuevo	Dock Sud	Total
1995	504,630	133,643	638,273
1996	530,346	249,208	779,554
1997	721,671	307,910	1,029,581
1998	818,334	363,703	1,182,037
1999	727,969	351,335	1,079,304
2000	735,107	367,082	1,102,189

Sources: Produced by the author based on data published by *Anuario Portuario y Marítimo*, (1996, 1998, 1999, and 2000) and statistics from AGP (2001).

Table 3: Buenos Aires and Dock Sud ports. Container movement (TEUs)

The Relationship between Puerto Madero and Puerto Nuevo

The relationship between Puerto Madero and Puerto Nuevo has been conflictual since the beginning. Puerto Madero, built at the end of the nineteenth century, and Puerto Nuevo, built at the beginning of the twentieth century, represent the partial materialization of two projects that confronted each other for over a decade: one by Eduardo Madero and the other by Luis Huergo; this history is outlined by Scobie and Silvestri, albeit with different interpretations.[8] The project by Madero was approved in 1882, and construction was completed in 1898. Its operation limitations resulted in the construction of a new port, with a design similar to the proposal by Huergo, although differing in location (to the north of Puerto Madero, and not in La Boca in the Riachuelo). The first establishments in Puerto Nuevo were opened in 1926. Since then, it has concentrated an increasing proportion of the port's movement, and Puerto Madero began to decay slowly. This decay accelerated in the 1980s with the increased use of containers, because it was not equipped for this new technology.

In 1989 the corporation Corporación Antiguo Puerto Madero was created and the transfer of land previously owned by the Administración General de Puertos initiated. The port enterprises and workers were initially against the transfer of land. In the negotiations between CAPM and the operators, it was agreed that for two years port activity would continue in a small area to the east of dock 4. Meanwhile, guided by the Ley de Puertos, the terminals of Puerto Nuevo and Dock Sud were put out for bids, and therefore the Puerto Madero land was no longer needed for the port's activity.

The relationship between the renovated port and the working port continues to present conflicting aspects:

1. The decision to find new uses for Puerto Madero implied taking away from the Buenos Aires port an area that could have been used for the movement of containers. This activity was displaced to several different points within the metropolitan area.

2. The working areas of Puerto Nuevo generate intense activity of loading vehicles. The trucks that

Operation	Original use	Final use	Parties involved	State of completion
Concession of terminals in Puerto Nuevo	Port	Port	National government Private concessionaries (license holders)	Completed (1994)
Dredging and extension of Puerto Nuevo	Port	Port Several (tertiary, residential, green space)	National government Private concessionaries	Postponed (1999)
Transfer of Dock Sud to the Province of Buenos Aires and concession of a container terminal	Port	Port	National government State/Province government Private concessionary (Exolgan)	Completed (1993)
Construction of a cruise terminal in Antepuerto Norte or Darsena Norte	Port	Port (passengers)	National government Government of the City of Buenos Aires (GCBA) Private concessionary	Under study
Privatization of the ex-shipyard Tandanor and development of the "Puerto Retiro" Project in Darsena Norte	Port-industrial	Offices Residential Tertiary Green space	National government (land sales) Private owners (land acquisition, project development) GCBA (approval or rejection)	Private project (under study)
Operations in Darsena Sur	Port and others	Not defined	National government GCBA	Indefinite
Retiro Area Project Retiro-Port Project	Railroad transportation	Railroad transportation Diverse urban uses	National government GCBA Railroad concessionaries Port concessionaries Architects Professional Assoc. (SCA)	Project
N-S railroad connection	Railroad transportation	Railroad transportation and others	National government GCBA Corp. Antiguo Puerto Madero (CAPM) Railroad concessionaries Owners in Puerto Madero	Project
Highways (BsAs-La Plata, Illia, 25 de Mayo)	Several	Automobile circulation Several under highway	National government GCBA (AUSA) Province of Buenos Aires Highway concessionaries	Completed (1980s and 1990s)
Riverside/Coastline Highway	Several (according to layout)	Indefinite (according to layout)	National government GCBA CAPM Highway concessionaries Owners in Puerto Madero	Project under discussion
Recovery of the Constanera Sur avenue	Circulation Green space	Circulation Green space	GCBA CAPM	Completed (since 1996)
Ecological Reserve improvements	Green space	Green space	GCBA NGOs	Completed (since 1996)
Urban renewal in San Telmo and La Boca	Several	Several	GCBA Real estate owners Construction companies, real estate companies, etc.	Varies (some complete, others at project stage)
Construction of office buildings in areas near Puerto Madero (Catalinas Norte, Madero-Huergo axis, etc.)	Several	Tertiary	GCBA (urban code) Private companies (owners, contractors, developers, etc.)	Varies (some complete, others at project stage)
Establishment of other tertiary activities in areas near Puerto Madero	Several	Tertiary	GCBA (urban code) State (several levels) Private companies	Varies (some complete, others at project stage)
Floating casino	Port	Recreational	National government GCBA Concessionary	In operation (since 1999)

Table 4: Completed or proposed interventions in coastal areas of the city of Buenos Aires (Even when beyond the boundaries of the city of Buenos Aires, Dock Sud is included given that until 1993 it was part of a single operational and institutional unit with the Buenos Aires port.)

Luis Javier Domínguez Roca

Type of operation	Operation or project	Relationship with Puerto Madero
Reconversion port-port	Privatization of Puerto Nuevo (concession of terminals to private operators)	Conflicting Areas of conflict: • Circulation of load trucks in Costanera Sur avenue • Traffic congestion in access roads to port due to private automobile circulation
	Dredging and extension of Puerto Nuevo	Conflicting • Worsening of conflicts generated by the port • Competing uses with Puerto Madero • Possible partial benefits with riverside/coastline highway resolution
	Operations in Darsena Sur	Indefinite
	Transfer of Dock Sud to the Province of Buenos Aires and concession to private operators	Neutral • Dock Sud absorbs part of the Buenos Aires port movement, contributing to the reduction of conflict in Puerto Nuevo • At the same time, part of the trips it generates pass near Puerto Madero
	Construction of a cruise terminal in Antepuerto Norte or Darsena Norte	Neutral • Positive aspects: the activities located in Puerto Madero would benefit from the influx of tourists with high purchasing power, the Terminal would benefit from Puerto Madero's urban image • Negative aspects: traffic congestion problems around Darsena Norte would worsen
Reconversion port-city	Privatization of the ex-shipyard Tandanor "Puerto Retiro" Project	Neutral • This project benefits from external influence generated by Puerto Madero, and competes for investments • Should it be completed it could worsen traffic congestion in Puerto Madero
Construction or renovation of transportation infrastructure	Project Retiro-Port	Neutral • The improvement of railroad access to Puerto Nuevo may improve traffic circulation in Puerto Madero • See Retiro Area Project
	N-S railroad connection	Positive (with the condition that the connection be done under ground)
	BsAs-La Plata Highway 25 de Mayo Highway Illia Highway	Positive • Improves accessibility of Puerto Madero at the metropolitan scale
	Riverside/Coastline Highway	Neutral • Improves accessibility of Puerto Madero at the metropolitan scale • It may partially channel through traffic, reducing conflicts in automobile circulation • It may generate visual or circulation "cutting effects" between Puerto Madero and the central area
Change in use of transportation infrastructure	Retiro Area Project	Neutral • The success of Puerto Madero leads the development of other operations such as the Retiro Area project • These operations may result in competing ones with Puerto Madero • The renovation of railroad layouts may benefit circulation in Puerto Madero
Recovery of green spaces	Recovery of the Constanera Sur Avenue	Positive The operation was undertaken through an agreement between the Government of the City of Buenos Aires (GCBA) and Corporación Antiguo Puerto Madero (CAPM)
	Ecological Reserve improvements	Positive
Rehabilitation of residential areas	Urban renewal in San Telmo and La Boca	Neutral (simultaneously competing and synergistic)
Specific undertakings	Construction of office buildings in areas near Puerto Madero (Catalinas Norte, Madero-Huergo axis, etc.)	Positive • The successful development of Puerto Madero leads these undertakings • The investments are complementary and not competing with Puerto Madero • They improve the image of the area
	Establishment of other tertiary activities in areas near Puerto Madero	
	Floating casino (in Darsena Sur)	Neutral • It generated jurisdiction conflicts • It brings visitors to the area • It may generate traffic congestion in access routes to Puerto Madero

Table 5: Relationships between Puerto Madero development and other interventions in coastal areas of the city of Buenos Aires (Even though beyond the boundaries of the city of Buenos Aires, Dock Sud is included given that until 1993 it was part of a single operational and institutional unit with the Buenos Aires port.)

circulate to and from the south must go through Puerto Madero, generating negative effects for circulation and the urban environment. The completion of the planning of the coastline highway may help to mitigate these effects, but it will be unable to eliminate them. Furthermore, the increasing number of private vehicles generated by activities in Puerto Madero also tends to obstruct access to Puerto Nuevo.

3. The delay in transferring the jurisdiction of the working port to the city administration implies that the city has no decision-making power over aspects of port activity that affect urban space.

In parallel to these conflicts are cooperative relationships and potential synergy between the activities of both areas. One example is the location of river passenger terminals in Dársena Norte, within port jurisdiction, but very near the offices and restaurants of the renovated port. Also, the possible location of a cruise terminal in this area is under study.

The Relationship between Puerto Madero and Other Interventions in the Coastal Area

The renovation of Puerto Madero is the most important intervention developed in the coastal areas of the city during the 1990s, but it is not the only one. Other operations backed by public or private interests may affect the future development of the area. Table 4 provides a tentative list of actions completed or planned for areas in proximity to Puerto Madero. For each, the changes in land use, involved parties, and current state of development is indicated. In table 5, the interventions are classified according to type and possible impact (positive, negative, or neutral) on the development of Puerto Madero. This table reflects the belief that the connection between the development of Puerto Madero and other projects located in neighboring areas are positive when one of the following conditions is met: 1) improvement of accessibility and circulation, 2) support for the development of new activities in adjacent areas, 3) location of green spaces, tertiary activities, and residential uses in neighboring areas, or 4) cooperation among organizations in charge of the projects.

At the same time, sources of negative impact would be: 1) traffic, particularly circulation of loading vehicles,

Eastern side, silos to be recovered

2) limitations to sightlines or circulation, 3) competition among activities located in neighboring areas, 4) jurisdictional conflicts between authorities. Finally, neutral impacts occur when there is a competition between activities located in the areas of the different interventions, or when there is a combination of both positive and negative impacts.

The Keys to Success and Future Risks

The Puerto Madero development is usually considered a successful operation. The project has generated new values for urban use, including an important allotment of public space, in an area previously abandoned and deteriorated. The creation of these use values supports the development of exchange values by private companies that have participated in the project, as well as by state and city governments through the corporation CAPM. However, only the development of the west area (45 hectares) has been completed; in the east

(95 hectares), the parcels that were to become private have been sold and many constructions are in advanced stages of development. The basic infrastructure has been built and some establishments are operating, among them a Hilton Hotel. But many office and apartment buildings are still under construction. As a result, it is not yet possible to do a rigorous evaluation of the whole operation. I will nonetheless try to identify the elements that have enabled the successful development that the project has had, as well as the risks that it will have to face in the future. In both cases, I will give special consideration to the connections between Puerto Madero and its local, national, and regional context.

From the forgoing analysis, one can highlight four types of elements: [9]

1. Economic and political context. Economic and institutional stability. Economic growth (particularly at the launching stage, 1991–94). Ample disposition of capital (national and foreign). Consensus

about the project between national and local political authorities.

2. Characteristics of the project area. Direct connection with the central area of the city. Accessibility. Continuity with the existing urban grid. Availability of land without use or with a low intensity of use. Availability of public land for development. Existence of buildings of historical or architectural value. Capacity for easy extension of service infrastructures. Landscape and environmental potential.

3. Project content. Combination of complementary uses, capable of acting synergistically. Definition of a scheme of public spaces (green, traffic, pedestrian, etc.) as a general development framework for the area. Definition of "key actions," structuring the operation in space and time.

4. Administration model. Definition of a responsible body, with the necessary autonomy and resources to carry through the project. Definition of a self-financing scheme. Elaboration of a master plan as general framework for the development of the area. Development in stages to achieve a favorable impact of initial interventions both in economic and symbolic terms, and a prudent distribution of costs and risks over time, allowing adaptation of project development to market responses. Elaboration of strategies to reach a reasonable degree of consensus among various state levels and sectors of civil society. Existence of favorable conditions for negotiation with the few preexisting private owners and other users of the area. Elaboration of a code adequate to the development of the plan.

What Problems and Threats Will It Have to Confront in the Future?

When considering the elements that have influenced the successful development of Puerto Madero, I place those that refer to the economic and political context first. That context was profoundly transformed in 2001.[10]

From 1988 there was a deep economic recession in Argentina. Even so, Puerto Madero continued to develop without major changes. One possible explanation is that the project was well advanced, and many investments were already agreed upon when the extent of the recession became evident. A situation that could be characterized as "dynamic inertia" took place: the project continued to develop steadily in spite of the unfavorable context. However, during the southern spring of 2001, the group IRSA—one of the main investors in the area—announced the delay of one of its projects for dock 4. Other projects have also been delayed.

By November 2001, the recession had become a pronounced depression, and it was combined with a massive withdrawal of bank deposits. The national government established restrictions on the availability of deposits, seriously affecting the holders of savings. Initially these policies did not affect the development of Puerto Madero. On the contrary, some investors decided to use their funds to buy real estate.

Between December 2001 and January 2002, the conditions that had propelled the development of Puerto Madero during the initial years had completely changed:

Economic and institutional stability: Generalized popular demonstrations led to President de la Rúa resigning from his post. In less than one month, five different leaders occupied the executive office. Payment of the country's external debt was suspended, as was the convertibility scale that tied the Argentine peso to the U.S. dollar. There was currency devaluation and the onset of spiraling inflation.

Economic growth: The generalized economic depression got worse. Unemployment rose to more than 20 percent of the active population. More than 50 percent of the total population was living below the poverty line.

Capital availability: The flight of deposits was followed by an almost total immobility of deposits remaining in the banking system. The trust of investors disappeared, and the influx of foreign capital was reversed.

Consensus: Earlier I referred to the consensus about the project among state authorities at various levels. The crisis did not influence this specific consensus, but it damaged the social legitimacy of all political authorities, a situation well expressed in the chant of demonstrators: "They should all leave!" Within this context, all public policies find it difficult to reflect consensus. This

Luis Javier Domínguez Roca

is manifest, for example, in the rejection of the Plan Urbano Ambiental de la Ciudad de Buenos Aires by several nongovernmental organizations. Arguing that there had not been enough public participation in the development of the plan, they were able to delay indefinitely its review by the city council.

But will this dramatic situation have consequences for Puerto Madero? The operation is nearing completion: the land has been sold, the planned infrastructures have been built to a large extent, and the private investments in real estate cannot be undone easily. The crisis had an important impact on demand for both offices and apartments, and the fall in consumer interest damages the commercial activity that has characterized the development of the west area (restaurants, bars, etc.). Even though this reduction in demand can slow the final stages of development, it is hard to imagine that it could undermine existing activities. In fact, although the economic, political, and social contexts have changed, the local spatial conditions that gave rise to this project still exist: proximity to the central area, accessibility, strong real estate value, landscape and environmental potential, etc.

In this sense, it is worth highlighting once again the strategic character of the adopted administration model: the organization of the process in stages, envisioning from the beginning the possibility of quicker or slower development depending on a host of factors. Spatial and temporal opportunities seized at the beginning of the project imprinted it with a dynamic that was difficult to stop despite years of recession and the so-called *corralito*.[11] On the other hand, it is possible that in the relatively near future, a stronger presence of foreign capital might be felt in Puerto Madero, as a consequence of the devaluation of the Argentine peso, the decrease in local demand, and the depreciation of land value relative to the international market.

In spite of the locational advantages of the Puerto Madero area, some unresolved aspects may bring difficulties in the near future. Most of these potential problems are related to transportation and circulation.[12]

1. There is conflict between lightweight traffic and trucking with origin or destination points in Puerto Madero.

2. The location of the so-called coastline highway initially planned for an area in the western part of Puerto Madero, between the project area and the traditional downtown of the city, has not been finalized. Such a highway could help decrease the conflict between local and through-traffic, but it could also generate negative effects. The type and magnitude of these effects depends on the route selected and its characteristics (elevated, ground level, or underground).

3. The development of the east area will generate several routes with origins or destination points there, which could result in traffic congestion in Puerto Madero and its environs.

4. There is no defined public transportation system for the east area.

The Appropriation of Value

Beyond the strictly urbanistic, some questions about the distribution of benefits from this project are pending:

- What is the total income obtained by the public sector through the Corporación Antiguo Puerto Madero?
- What income has the private sector obtained?
- To what purpose have successive national and local administrations put the income?
- The municipal ordinance that established the zoning of the west sector in 1991 required the local administration to assign for housing, education, and health the income arising from its participation in CAPM. Has this rule been complied with?
- The Puerto Madero infrastructure has been built using income obtained by CAPM land sales. Who will finance its maintenance, once CAPM meets its goals and is dissolved?

These questions imply considering the benefits received by various groups in evaluating the operation, beyond its success or failure in strictly real estate terms.

Notes

1. Luis Javier Domínguez Roca, "Dynamique urbaine et restructuration portuaire: le cas de Buenos Aires," in *CERUR. Notes de Recherche, Documents de Travail, Etudes* 8, 1999. Centre d'Etudes et de Recherches Urbaines et Régionales (CERUR), Paris.

2. TEU stands for "twenty-foot equivalent unit," or the measure of capacity of a 20-foot container.

3. The revitalization project of the oceanfront of Rio de Janeiro from the Santos Dumont airport to the Candelaria church was approved by the municipal council in 1997 and may be added to a public space renovation policy developed since 1993, under the name "Rio Cidade." This area of the coastline corresponds to the historical, commercial, and administrative center. Located there are the navy's installations, an abandoned passenger terminal, and a tertiary dock that were not reached by the renovation process. The project's goal is to substantially transform circulation and eliminate the barrier that vehicular traffic represents for public access to coastal areas. It also proposes the creation or rehabilitation of attractions in the area, for both residents and potential visitors. The project includes the following steps: move more traffic underground, maintain in use the elevated lane of the perimeter avenue, locate restaurants and spaces under this avenue with views toward the city and the ocean, build housing and hotels, establish a large shopping mall in the passenger terminal, expand cultural offerings through the construction of an aquarium, a museum in the airport, and another museum in the Dock de la Armada.

4. The Plan Fénix is a national program financed by the InterAmerican Development Bank for the revitalization of cities. In the case of La Aguada, the first stage provides for the liberation of lands previously used by the railroad, the renovation of buildings located along that land, the concession of the Estación Central for a cultural and commercial center, and the building of a new passenger railroad terminal. Also under construction is an "intelligent" tower of 170 meters for the offices of the Agencia Nacional de Telecomunicaciones.

5. L. J. Domínguez Roca and F. A. Arias, "Privatización y cambio tecnológico en el puerto de Buenos Aires: su impacto en el espacio urbano," in *Actas del IV Encuentro de Geógrafos de América Latina*, Buenos Aires, 1997.

6. Carlos Armero Sisto, ed., *Anuario Portuario y Marítimo*, Buenos Aires, 1996.

7. *La Razón*, Rutas y Transportes supplement, September 12, 1996, p. 3.

8. James Scobie, *Buenos Aires, del Centro a los Barrios 1870–1910* (Buenos Aires: Solar, 1986); Graciela Silvestri, "La ciudad y el río," in Jorge Francisco Liernur and Graciela Silvestri, *El umbral de la metrópolis: Transformaciones técnicas y cultura en la modernización de Buenos Aires (1870–1930)* (Buenos Aires: Sudamericana, 1993), pp. 97–176.

9. This listing is based on a previous work (Alvarado and Domínguez 1998).

10. The first version of this work was completed in July 2001; this point has been reformulated in May 2002.

11. *Corralito* is the term that some journalists used to refer to restrictions on the availability of bank deposits; this expression was widely used, even by members of the administration's economic team.

12. Some of these problems have been discussed in a previous work; see Luis Javier Domínguez Roca, "Reciclaje de puertos, accesibilidad, circulación: el caso de Puerto Madero," in *Cuadernos de Territorio 9*, Universidad de Buenos Aires, Facultad de Filosofía y letras, Instituto de Geografía, 1997.

The Puerto Madero Competition
and Urban Ideas in Buenos Aires in the 1980s

Adrián Gorelik

Puerto Madero has a special place in the urban history of Buenos Aires. Throughout the modern history of the city, it has served as the major test site for models and proposals that offered varied visions not only for the port but also for the city and the roles of the urban and of architecture. This happened again in the 1980s when, after decades of neglect, the port became the protagonist of a process of cultural and urban recovery that ended in the establishment of the Corporación Antiguo Puerto Madero and the competition of ideas for its strategic planning, between 1989 and 1991. Should one focus only on that peak moment, one might think that Puerto Madero was simply another in a series of operations that could be characterized as "urbanism on demand" that became common internationally during those years. Puerto Madero was indeed the first—and probably the only—successful expression of those new

trends in Buenos Aires. But to understand what modalities it adopted in this city, and what transformations it prompted in its urban and architectural culture, the composition of the new climate of ideas that developed during the decade should be analyzed.

Archeologies of Modernity

The port was the main element to embody that new climate of ideas: all prior proposals for its transformation had been based on its technical obsolescence; but during the 1980s it was precisely that obsolescence that provided new value to the port as a cultural testimony of modernity. Rather than postmodernism, the urban culture of Buenos Aires fostered a sort of postdevelopment modernity. It was marked by the passage from a modernizing to a modernist vision of technique; the nostalgic and archeological recovery of a "classical modernity" that had begun precisely with the construction of the port in the 1880s and ended in the architectural avant-garde

Puerto Madero, final plan

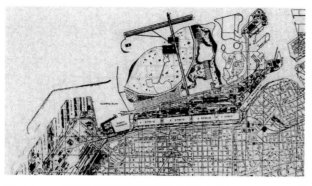

of the 1930s and 1940s. A generic climate of ideas favored the inarticulate coexistence of a multitude of views from the international debate. And although it would be completely shaped only in the second half of the 1980s, with the establishment of democracy, this framing of the port began at the beginning of the decade. In 1977, the military government organized an international bid to develop Puerto Madero into a land business that—although it failed—signaled the incubation of a more ambitious agenda. This project was the landfill of 400 hectares along the city front that sought to materialize in the port area the proposals of the modernist development tradition, based on city-planning proposals put forward since 1958. The revival of that project, however, supported a series of experimental initiatives that led in a completely different direction.

Two main visions for the site originated in 1980: the understanding of the port as an "urban piece" independent of a global plan, and the architectural valuing of its oldest buildings. These ideas imply important changes for the port and for the urban and architectural culture. They arose from design studio exercises in La Escuelita, a significant institution at the time.[1] In 1980, Justo Solsona developed in his architectural design studio the theme "400 hectares in the river" as a project "for a nonexistent site." Although his proposal is for a program no less development oriented than the official plan, the formal character of the work produced in the course shows that the traditional diagnosis was simply

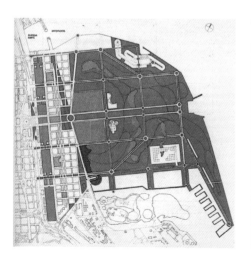

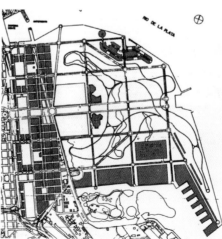

Puerto Madero competition
(Tony Diaz, Luis Ibarlucia, Roberto Gil, Daniel Silberfaden, Manuel Fernandez de Luco)

20 Ideas for Buenos Aires competition, areas of intervention

Ensanche del Area Central plan
(M.R. Alvarez, R. Raña Veloso, R.H. Alvarez, S. Forster, F.H. Serra, J.O. Valera)

Adrián Gorelik

taken as springboard for design possibilities. What surprises in the exercise of La Escuelita is its bluntness in terms of the geometric definition of urban forms. In opposition to the abstract way it had been treated in previous plans, the port was now viewed as the object of systematic design thought. And in that design thought the urban grid dominates. The value of that structure of repetition was "discovered" after more than a century of repudiation on the part of urban and architectural thought.[2] Putting aside the somewhat playful character of the exercise, it shows that in a fragmentary consideration of the city, a collage of architectural artifacts was being dealt with. This point of view presupposed (and was allowed by) a new understanding of the urban, with emphasis on the architectural over the urbanistic.

The second novel idea was the appreciation of the architectural patrimony, something particularly evident in the competition for the redesign of one of the old warehouses of the port as student housing, organized by La Escuelita at the end of 1980. With the exception of a passing mention in EDA2000, previous proposals for the port eliminated all of its old installations. A new conservationist climate was slowly emerging, although its relationship with the military dictatorship was complex. Because the dictatorship embodied the most authoritarian aspects of modernizing planning—exemplified in the construction of highways that demolished wide bands of the city—a new alignment began to appear between conservationist preoccupations and anti-dictatorial critique.

Two projects that shared first prize expressed quite different interpretations: in one case, the preoccupation with history was concrete and tangible, though limited to the architectural shell; in the other, it was conceptual and abstract, disassembling the building to recreate within it the typology of the blocks of the urban grid—history as a new urban scenography, or history as a dense grid on which to produce infinite associations. But within the framework of restricted debate necessitated by the dictatorship, the reduction from city to architecture could not but make the urban issue superficial; this was the main limitation of these kinds of approaches. The lack of discussion of the city in all of its cultural, political, social, technical, and economical complexity

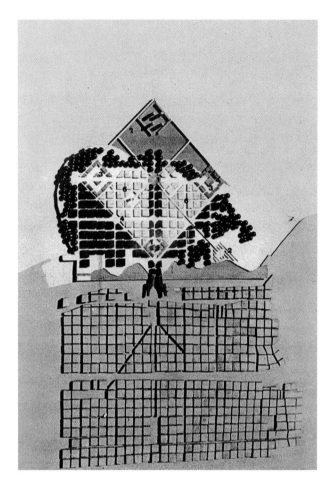

Plan from La Escuelita

meant a failure to account for the immediate past. It transformed the integrity of previously undertaken, imagined, and materialized interventions into a stratified superposition of uncommunicated experiences.

Central Area Extension: Compromise between Modernization and Modernism

After some unsuccessful proposals, the dictatorship decided to assign, in 1981, the Desarrollo Urbanístico Ensanche Area Central (EAC), or central area extension, to a team of professionals connected to traditional development planning and others familiar with the new trends seen in La Escuelita, dividing tasks between "city planning program" and "urban design."[3]

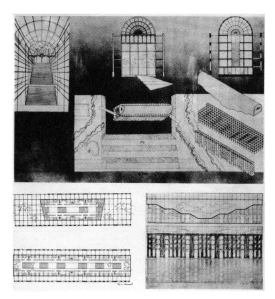

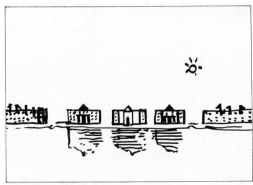

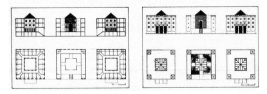

First prize, Concurso Galpones (Gloria Benbassat)

First prize, Concurso Galpones (Pablo Carpman)

The program emerged from an analysis of the city that supported the diagnosis of previous urban master plans: it proposed the total removal of all port activities, a complete urbanization of the area (167 hectares, which in a little more than thirty years could reach 5,300,000 square meters of dense construction, to accommodate 130,000 tertiary-sector employees and provide housing for 48,000 residents), and the construction of a landfill for a metropolitan park of more than 450 hectares.[4] The park idea constituted another step toward the tradition of expanding green areas that is analyzed in other chapters of this book. The proposal for the tertiary sector sought to address two needs highlighted by the general diagnosis: to satisfy future demands for employment and to recover the traditional centralized structure of the city. The symptoms of eroded structure were evident in the distortion of residential use in the northern area of downtown, which appeared colonized by tertiary use. EAC sought to correct such distortions by recovering the role of Avenida de Mayo as the central axis of the city, in agreement with the regulated transformation of the southern neighborhood that had already taken place.[5]

The urban design itself shows the harmony of EAC with the new trends expressed in the projects of La Escuelita: the privileged location of Puerto Madero was used to provide it with a solution full of references to the existing city. The most explicit symmetry was added by the use of gridded blocks, which materialized the continuity within the port of the Avenida de Mayo axis and dissolved the asymmetry given by the Costanera Sur in what seemed a play of mirrors along the axis.

The project could be read, then, as a convenient compromise between different trends. But the separation of tasks implied less of a departure from the planning tradition than limits to the development possibilities of a new understanding of "urban design." Traditional planning was better able to work with the modernizing authoritarianism of the military government than was the new urbanism.

Public Space and Monument: Urbanistic Ideas between Democracy and the Crisis

Public space was fully introduced into the urban discourse in 1983. Public space in the new context was transformed into the backdrop of a sort of urban democratic ritual that provided continuity to the antidictatorial struggle, bringing together the most varied expressions of celebration and protest.[6] The other

Adrián Gorelik

transformation was that the new democratic governments shelved the projects that assumed large public investments. Projects that had previously appeared as the natural continuity of urban development were regarded derisively as "pharaonic." What became fundamental was the idea of "city by parts," which allowed a dismissal of the structural ambitions of the traditional plans: the new vision of the city, as a mosaic of different situations, offered not only a pluralistic perspective in terms of breaking from totalizing (read: totalitarian) illusions of the modernizing city but also a realistic reading inasmuch as it supported the execution of small, fragmentary projects.

Little was done in any case in the port: some entrances were distributed along the fence, and public access to the municipal waterfront of the Costanera Sur was encouraged. This traditional place for urban leisure appeared reconquered by democracy. Suddenly it was discovered that in the landfill area, a peculiar new landscape was being formed. It reproduced aspects of the flora and fauna of the Paraná in the gaps between the rubble from demolitions undertaken by the dictatorship to clear room for highways. This area became the "Ecological Reserve."

The postdevelopment modernist sensibility supported in limited circles since the end of the 1970s found in the combination of political democracy and economic crisis the condition for its dissemination with a new common meaning. Its major outcome in urban terms was the call for proposals, "Ideas Urbano-Arquitectónicas para Buenos Aires," known as "20 Ideas," in 1986, with the purpose of devising significant architectural interventions in twenty "urban voids." New understandings finding expression in Europe (urban cultural identity as source rather than product of social identity, decentralization as synonym of participation and democracy, public space as imbued with political and economic character) spread among the architects. These same architects became the main actors in the design of the city, with the market and civil society as promoters and users.[7]

The port was one of the main "voids" selected. Identified as "Ensanche Area Central y Costanera" (widening of the central area and coastal areas), it reflected the ambiguous continuity with the program

Model, competition of ideas for Puerto Madero (Clorindo Testa, Maria Jorcino de Aguilar, Alberto Mizrahi, Claudia Rispo)

Drawing, competition of ideas for Puerto Madero (Borghini-Hojman-Hojman-Minond-Pereyra-Pschepiurca)

Model, competition of ideas for Puerto Madero (Borthagaray-Gastellu-Marre)

favored by the dictatorship. But against such continuity, Tony Díaz led the response that radicalized the new cultural sensibility.[8] His project did not affect the triangle of the old Puerto Madero, but concentrated the whole intervention toward the east of the Costanera Sur and reduced it to a minimal gesture: two lines that cross. The main one was a new coastline-pier on the river, while the landfill area was recovered as a coastline park. In opposition to the developmental vision, the proposal denied any possible "continuity" between the port and the city: the port, he affirmed, must maintain its quality as an exceptional place. Furthermore, the port was transformed into monument: it was simply about capitalizing on the richness of the obsolete industrial landscape, countering the archeological view that the renovation projects had initiated. The team led by Díaz did not propose a renovation, because the port is not just any monument. It reminds us of an industrial past that never was, one of the truncated future pasts of the country and the city. Therefore the decision to intervene by not intervening in the port for the first time called into question the organic relationship between planning and development. In such a way, not only was the developmental diagnosis questioned, but the "20 Ideas" were formalized without a new general diagnosis of the city, unlike the Spanish case that inspired them. Still, Puerto Madero was one of the favorite topics of academic projects at the time. The design course of the first democratically elected dean of the architecture school, Juan Manuel Borthagaray, developed the most systematic approach.[9] The study offered a diagnosis rather than a design solution—a comprehensive survey of the buildings and infrastructure, the fragmentation of new domains, and the flora and fauna now living in the landfill. It also called attention to the barrier that would have been created by the coastline highway had the elevated route planned by the Dirección Nacional de Vialidad been built. One of its main innovations was to apply to the area not the general ideological vocabulary of the new urbanism, but—though timidly—the battery of concepts that Peter Hall calls the urbanism "of developers."[10] The proposal includes financial engineering, although it clearly differs from North American examples in that it prioritizes the public interest as expressed in the type of bids assigned to private hands for construction and use during a specified time, without transfer of buildings or land. The study proposed an autonomous entity for administration and the formulation of flexible plans.

From Corporation to Master Plan: The Arrival of Developers

As shown, toward the mid-1980s many new urban planning ideas had emerged on the scene. Yet debates within disciplines continued to take place in a world disassociated from the real construction of the city. Everything remained the same in the port, and toward the end of the decade the cycle of hyperinflation that doomed Raul Alfonsin's administration led to a state of crisis, where it seemed impossible to even think about urban interventions of any kind.

It was precisely then, however, that the transformation began. Carlos Grosso, the mayor of the city assigned by the new president, Carlos Menem, seemed to have taken to heart one of the stock management phrases beloved by "strategic planning": the moment of maximum crisis is the moment of maximum opportunity. And Puerto Madero was the "grand project" through which to readdress, from deep within the urban crisis, new dynamics for growth. An operation of this magnitude was made possible to a great extent thanks to society's paralysis, which eliminated obstacles for the administration.[11] Alfredo Garay, the planning director of the administration, was largely responsible for the organization of the Puerto Madero operation; he became aware of the changes that needed to be implemented to introduce the urbanism of developers to Buenos Aires—to transform the state as the avant-garde of the new type (and new scale) of private business within the city.

But to lead such a process of change, it was first necessary to unlock the main obstacle that the port presented to its own transformation: the entanglement of jurisdictions. To address this problem, in 1989 the Corporación Antiguo Puerto Madero was formed. It was one of the few successful institutional coordination initiatives in the history of Buenos Aires. Providing continuity with the agreements that had been initiated with the

Adrián Gorelik

Spanish urban teams, Consultores Europeos Asociados was commissioned to produce the master plan. Joan Busquets and Joan Alemany headed it, with significant participation in the form of others with experience in the urban planning of Barcelona, including consultants Jordi Borja, who was then in the city council. Supporting teams in Buenos Aires were led by Alfredo Garay and Jorge Moscato. Based on the continuity of the gridded block system of Buenos Aires—although without strict adherence to the existing layout—the project was presented under the title "Plan Estratégico de Antiguo Puerto Madero" in July 1990. Curiously, the plan assumed an almost literal return to the postulates of EAC and did not acknowledge the more radical positions adopted in "20 Ideas." Once again it was about reinforcing the city's centrality, producing an extension of the city over the port, guaranteeing continuity between the city and the new area. A schematic continuity of the gridded blocks and a transversal monumental axis were called for, as well as a return of the "lost equilibrium" by using the port as a pole for recentering and development, capable of transmitting uses and urban quality from the north toward the south. EAC was even recovered in terms of details, such as the proposed continuation of a subway line and adaptive reuse of the great warehouses. There were of course several differences: the disappearance of trust in the expansion of tertiary activity; the impossibility of intervening in the landfill (now Ecological Reserve); a greater liberty in the decision on size and form of blocks (proportionate to the decrease in interest in its typological study); a smaller buildable area (3,000,000 square meters as opposed to the 5,300,000 square meters of EAC). From a programmatic point of view, however, the main difference was that what in EAC had been the creation of an area for metropolitan use (in accord with the program of development planning) was transformed in the master plan into a simple extension of the city, the creation of a new "neighborhood" in Buenos Aires (according to the idea of supporting "strategic" areas for the development of urban business).

The main innovation of the master plan was not evident in the urban proposal, however, but in its vision of administration. They proposed a simple and efficient

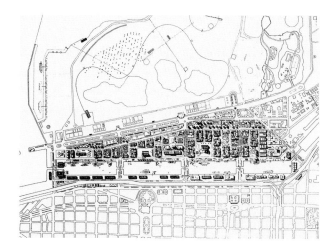

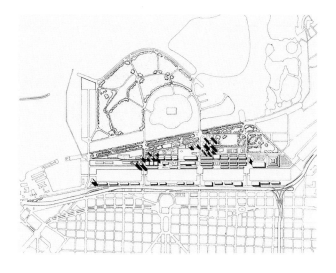

National competition of ideas for Puerto Madero, plans of three first-prize winners

Perspective, competition of ideas for Puerto Madero (Cristián Carnicer, Alejandro Labeur, Rómulo Pérez, Eugenio Xaus)

system of materializing a project that would offer a global image, but that could be broken down into operations of a controllable scale for private developers (placing emphasis on the fact that each phase included architectural projects and urban image). The Corporation would provide infrastructure and would sell not only "sites" but complete sectors of the project. It was an administration system with public initiative and control, with private involvement and financing activated as required, in the sense that the administration would set the priorities, the timing, and the scale of interventions.

In 1991 the city council approved legislation for the preservation of the architectural patrimony of the warehouses and invited bids for the first warehouses (those located between docks 3 and 4), with an incredible public response. The Corporation received decisive support from private investors, and the sale became symbolic of the opening of the port to civil society, with the elimination of the fences that had signaled its separation from the city.

From Debate to Competition: The Construction of Consensus

Meanwhile, the local architectural community, led by the architectural association Sociedad Central de Arquitectos, rejected the master plan. This stance represented a natural continuation of SCA's oppositional tradition: it had bravely opposed the military dictatorship, which brought it strong popular support. The SCA's position on Puerto Madero prompted a process of negotiation, from which the national open competition emerged. The SCA's objections to the master plan were basically twofold: the absence of a general urban plan where the port was taken into consideration, and the purely speculative character of the official project. Countering the SCA, the municipal officers boldly presented the master plan as the policy most in agreement with the popular ideology of Peronism, in that it would recover the downtown and therefore strengthen the impoverished south.

Three positions in the debate would lead to programmatic compromise for the competition. First was traditional planning, as voiced by architect and urban planner Odilia Suárez, featuring three premises: port uses should be guaranteed; the whole area should be used mainly for central administration and leisure; and residential use should be merely complementary.

The second position was that of the Secretaría de Planeamiento Municipal, or municipal planning office. It held onto the structural goals of the master plan, presenting it not as a project but as the formulation of alternative scenarios for administrative engineering—not an urban-architectural model but a platform for investment, a public-private joint venture. Precisely because it was a scheme that could be continuously modified in its specifics, following a non-negotiable model of urban intervention, Garay had no problem in dismissing the master plan as urban project as long as the competition include in its requirements the keys of the administration process.

The third position was that of the design architects already trained in the rejection of traditional planning. They had specific critiques of the master plan as urban project but, above all, they wanted to participate in the initiative through an urban competition and through the construction of buildings. This is why, as was well interpreted by SCA, they were ready to concede more general discussions.

This is how an agreement between SCA and the municipal administration was reached, resulting in a request for proposals in June 1991. All parties involved in the professional debate greeted this advance with relief. The preparation of the competition requirements assumed, once again, a compromise among different tendencies: traditional planning represented by consultants assigned by SCA, and "developer's urbanism" represented by those assigned by the municipality; the compromise was built around the idea of "recovery of the downtown." In such a way, the planning tradition could consider that its old general plan for the city was maintained, while the municipal administration would relate the downtown objective to the "popular" character of the initiative. At the same time, that idea allowed the recovery of the notion of modernization—a premise never revised by the planning tradition, which was also the basis for the official project for the city and more generally of the vision shaped in the country during the 1990s.

The requirements for the competition could be understood as the programmatic translation of the analysis undertaken by Suárez; the premises of the request for proposals closely follow her arguments. The administration model operated within the framework put forward by the municipal administration for the "grand projects."[12] Neither the use of the Reserve nor the route of the

highway was considered; the competition was restricted to the edges of the triangle between the docks and the Costanera.

Viewing the design competition from this perspective, it is easy to understand the triumph of the team led by Juan Manuel Borthagaray (Borthagaray, Gastellu, Marré, Pérez Guimil, Rosellini, Doval, Behar, Coos, and Dietrich). This team expressed the consensus with greatest elegance, giving true form to the basic objectives of all parties involved.[13]

Puerto Madero and the Fragmentary Modernization of Buenos Aires

Puerto Madero started to materialize during the 1990s and offered the best evidence that Buenos Aires was recovering its urban dynamism. In this sense, the risk taken by Garay for the rest of his administration was to create a postcard image of Buenos Aires for the twenty-first century. The great contribution of the Corporation was the imagination and bravery with which it unlocked the area for its administration. But the Corporation failed to create mechanisms to enable the enormous gains in value obtained from that "invented"

Drawing, competition of ideas for Puerto Madero (Enrique Garcia Espil, Mariana Leidermann, Antonio Tufaro, Fabián Maci, Fernando Sabatini, Mariana Soldini)

area for the market to be used again in the rest of the city; the city has not benefited significantly from business deals it made with private interests in Puerto Madero.

Furthermore, the transformation of the area has not generated positive spillover effects for the most degraded areas of the city (the traditional downtown and the south). Neither did the innovations that we saw emerge in the urban ideas of the 1980s receive new energy from the Puerto Madero operation: on the contrary, the complete absence of debate that followed the competition is alarming.

On the other hand, Puerto Madero represented an advance in a modality of broad intervention that signaled an epochal shift in the Buenos Aires of the 1990s—the participation of important private capital in initiatives that affect urban sectors at a territorial scale. From it emerged the phenomenon of the "megaproject" on which urban modernization dynamics concentrated during the 1990s: the Retiro Project, the Abasto, the Tren de la Costa, and the metamorphosis of Tigre.

Puerto Madero provided a different incentive from that expected by those worried by the recentralization of the city. The creation of "megaprojects" has been fundamental to the emergence of a new model of decentralized city. In contrast to the traditional system of Buenos Aires, characterized by its "European" central

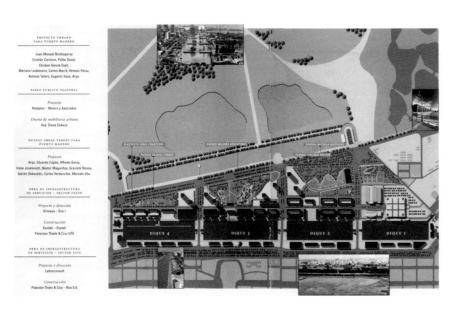

Strategic plan of Puerto Madero, 1990
(Consultores Europeos Asociados)

Strategic plan of Puerto Madero, 1990
(Consultores Europeos Asociados)

Adrián Gorelik

public space, what has developed is a system of Latin American modernization: a system of highways and malls, similar to North American suburbanization, but within the framework of the marked social differences of the Latin American city. Of course Puerto Madero is not itself responsible for this global change. But the policy of the urban fragment and the "grand projects" that had in Puerto Madero its moment of glory implicitly led to this result. Unlike what occurred in European cities, the logic of the fragment has worked in Buenos Aires as the urban counterpart of increasing social fragmentation.

Notes

1. La Escuelita was a private association for the teaching of architecture created and directed by Tony Díaz, Ernesto Katzenstein, Justo Solsona, and Rafael Viñoly between 1976 and 1983—the same years of the military dictatorship. The motive for its establishment preceded the coup d'état, however, and was not overtly political: a need to recover the most significant disciplinary elements of the architectural debate. But circumstance would lead to La Escuelita functioning as an alternative to the teaching of architecture as privileged by the dictatorship, as was being done at the Universidad de Buenos Aires.

2. Research on the gridded block structure by Tony Díaz in projects of La Escuelita was of fundamental importance to that rediscovery.

3. The hired consortium was comprised of the architectural offices of Mario Roberto Alvarez, Raña Veloso-Alvarez-Foster, and Serra Valera, three offices that had received many commissions from the military government, which they then subcontracted to smaller offices and prestigious figures within the profession. In such a way, a great portion of the public work done during the 1970s was undertaken. The EAC team included diverse tendencies. Representing the planning tradition, Juan Ballester Peña, who had been responsible for the Esquema Director para el Año 2000 done in 1969, and Odilia Suárez and Eduardo Sarrahil, responsible for the Plan Regulador 1958–62, were hired by the consortium to head the subgroup tackling "urban development and urbanistic programming." Standing for the architectural tradition, Ernesto Katzenstein was put in charge of the coordination of the whole study; his subgroup for "urban design" was comprised of several younger architects who had participated with him in La Escuelita and other designers also committed to new ideas.

4. The landfill proposal was complementary to the formation of the Cinturón Ecológico. The military government sought to create, also through landfills, a park that would encircle the metropolis and address the lack of green space in a growing city.

5. See, in this volume, "Puerto Madero: An Argentine History."

6. It was not only a theoretical issue: the massive occupation of streets and parks was a main characteristic of the democratic transition. Several initiatives joined art and politics to reclaim the collective use of the city. Human rights demonstrations, beginning in the last years of the dictatorship, had incorporated masks and street paintings to represent the *desaparecidos*; street theater, large-scale concerts, art biennales, and activities of new neighborhood centers all presented a vibrant, colorful city—in opposition to the "cleanliness" obsession of the dictatorship.

7. The name "20 Ideas" reveals the influence of European initiatives, as it was inspired by "50 Ideas para Madrid" and organized with the cooperation of Spanish urbanists. Although none of those "20 ideas" materialized, the competition provided dynamism to the disciplinary debate.

8. The project was taken up by Tony Díaz's design studio at the architecture school of the Universidad de Buenos Aires and included Díaz, Luis Ibarlucía, Roberto Gil, Daniel Silberfaden, and Manuel Fernández de Luco.

9. An agreement between the university and the transportation office of the public works ministry (with partial jurisdiction over the port) was signed in 1985; the architecture school was in charge of producing an analysis of the area's conditions and developing proposals for its development, tasks undertaken by Borthagaray's design studios during 1986 and 1987.

10. These concepts were applied with reference to the port experiences of Baltimore and Boston that, together with the more recent Docklands of London development, only started to be considered in Argentina by the mid-1980s.

11. Economic Emergency and State Reform laws gave President Menem's administration free rein to advance a radical deregulation of economic activity, with an emphasis on the privatization of services and public companies. Local political malfeasance further strengthened the president's hand.

12. Those who participated in the competition were to be capable of showing spatial schemes of growth for the different stages of the administration ("investment modules"). Special importance was given to the "character" of the proposal, a notion that was reduced to the *aggiornamento* of the "national and popular" tradition (transformed into a celebration of urban pop). In support of the traditional planning point of view, the buildable volume was reduced to 1,500,000 square meters, with 50 percent open space and accommodation for somewhat more than 7,000 residents; housing is defined as a "support to the promotion of the area and as a dignified accompaniment to tertiary activity, recreation, and patrimony preservation, for which it was primarily destined."

13. Its project strategy was to lay two rows of blocks along the east side of the docks, leaving the rest of the triangle as a park in dialogue with the Reserve. This was obtained thanks to the option of penetration of two axes from the city toward the river, through the streets Perón and Belgrano, which end in two clumps of towers in the green. This arrangement recovers the modernist model of towers in the park, recreating the classic Corbusian image.

On the Administration of Urban Projects:
The Lessons of Puerto Madero

Alfredo M. Garay

When our team was put in charge of the municipal administration in July 1989, we decided to implement a policy for recovering the downtown of Buenos Aires through several simultaneous lines of action. The first sought to materialize a "prestige" operation that would restore to the *porteño*[1] imagination the paradigm of the old downtown. Its main component was the revitalization program called Programa de Revitalización de la Avenida de Mayo (PRAM).[2] The second called for changes in the urban code, in the hope of channeling investments beyond the city's central area.[3] A third proposal advanced the renovation of buildings with historical value to serve as social housing, so as not to displace their inhabitants, who were mainly of modest income. With no tradition of this type of policy, three different approaches to occupied municipal buildings were supported (the city block known as San Francisco, the *conventillos* or tenements of La Boca,[4] and the Padelai building). In all cases, proposals presented by squatter occupants were considered. Last, the area of the old port presented itself as a great opportunity to incorporate a new area of urbanization downtown.

At the time, the country was going through a deep economic crisis, making it difficult to imagine this kind of initiative within the context of a recession. The Puerto Madero urbanization supported the urbanistic goals of recovering the relationship of the city with the river, providing a significant amount of green area, and restoring the residential character that the downtown had lost. It also helped to promote the development of new economic activities and employment.

Paradoxically, most of these objectives were mentioned among the intentions of urban plans developed in the last seventy years, which, for various reasons, were never implemented. Within the framework of an economic crisis, it was clear that effort had to be expended to materialize proposals, refining intervention mecha-

Eastern side of the docks

nisms through concrete programs. Overcoming inertia was a fundamental prerequisite to these operations that, furthermore, had to be simple (with a first stage of rapid materialization) and validated by a significant number of parties involved.

A consensus was reached on the need to implement programs for the recovery of historical centers, including the development of new alternatives for social housing (for example, by remodeling tenements). We believed that architects were our front-line allies.[5]

Port activity was also undergoing a serious crisis.[6] The first initiative of the municipal government was to evaluate the possibilities of the site, assigning a team from the planning office (Secretaría de Planeamiento) to develop, in a short time, a preliminary study.[7] The result was a matrix that related the quantity of sites and their possible construction and sales value with the cost of infrastructure, public space, and administration. An administration model was created based on the establishment of an urbanizing association that would generate its own financing. The operation therefore was to be accomplished without cost to the state; it was thought that it might actually produce funds that could finance other urban interventions.[8] Only one meeting with the country's president was necessary for him to approve the plan.

Establishing the Corporation

The Corporación Antiguo Puerto Madero (CAPM) was established with a six-member board of directors, four representing the national government and two representing the city government. It would provide the master plan and technical resources, and have the authority to assign value to land. Shareholders would audit the development of the Corporation through three trustees. Shareholders would meet once a year and the board of directors at least once a month; the presidency rotates yearly between the two government levels represented. A professional management body carries out the daily operation.[9]

Construction of Agreements

It was clear to us that it was not the moment to propose a new plan, but rather to follow through with pending proposals within a strategic framework.[10] A presidential decree allowed us to arrange a cooperation agreement with the city council of Barcelona, which was in the midst of renovating its own port and building accommodations for the Olympics.[11] With the input of Catalan architects[12] who interacted with the municipal team,[13] a more mature version of our plan was produced and used as a guide to develop the first phase of the enterprise.

Similarly, the presidential decree prompted wide discussion. Because there were no permanent residents on the site (a condition that contributed enormously to the viability of the project), popular opinion did not reflect, as in other cases, the reaction of people directly affected but of citizens who voiced their opinion with a certain level of generality.

The first to express their opinions were the port operators, vindicating the use of the docks as support areas. This gave us the opportunity to initiate a round of meetings to address the modernization of the operating port (Puerto Nuevo).[14] A second group argued that the whole site should be a park, because the downtown lacked green spaces. The third leading voice[15] was that of international real estate developers.[16] Donald Trump was the first to arrive, brought in by a local architect (at the time, the main shopping mall builder). He announced his visit to us through a press release, in which he showed plans and perspective drawings of his project for the urbanization of Puerto Madero.[17]

Almost all of the developers wanted us to transfer to them the control of the Corporation, allowing the private sector to take charge. They thought that the state was not capable of leading this type of intervention, or of bringing together the necessary investments. Confronted with such a demonstration of power, we considered it necessary to persevere in the idea of a state-owned corporation that would remain faithful to the political and urbanistic objectives of the project. International investors would not accept the offer to develop only a part of the project, much less only a building. They also expressed serious doubts about the

Alfredo M. Garay

Western side
of the docks

warranties the state could provide to each investor, calling into question its ability to have any impact on the quality of projects on adjacent sites.

We strengthened the hypothesis of the Corporation as a state-owned entity that took as its responsibility the urbanization of sites and confronted the commercializa-

tion of existing buildings and urbanized land. Although this narrowed our field of action, it made it much more concrete. We defined the location where land would begin to be sold, promoted the development of the more attractive parts of the program (those with greater capability for favorably affecting the environment south of

Old "Molinos Rio de la Plata" building (undergoing restoration)

the project), and established deadlines for the construction of buildings, avoiding speculative investors who would sit on empty land.

The Corporation took responsibility for building infrastructure, based on a detailed cash-flow plan that would guarantee financing. The Corporation's challenge was to gain credibility with prospective investors—trust that a state organization would efficiently invest proceeds of initial sales to finance the construction of infrastructure.

Feasibility studies were directed not so much to the assessment of whether there would be demand for apartments or offices in the city as to whether there were potential buyers of sites on which might be built an apartment or office building.

Buildings being built at the time followed precise typologies favored by companies that tended to specialize in a specific product. This understanding was fundamental when we exchanged ideas with the Catalan urban

Alfredo M. Garay

planners. Once the possible products were identified and the parameters taken into account when businesses selected a location, it was necessary to review the first master plan in search of a more versatile geometry that would allow a single site to respond to the needs of different products. The new proposal had to also offer sites to relatively small businesses, to increase the number of participants, without putting the economic goals of the project at risk.[18]

The historical experience of the city made it difficult to believe that a single economic group would develop the totality of the project,[19] or that several groups would be willing to share different parts of a single enterprise. So we decided to trust in the dynamics of smaller groups, reserving for the state the role of distributor. We had to assume the inherent lack of prestige of public organizations and the need to transfer functions to the private sector.

As the announcements became public, a fourth player joined the opposition: the Sociedad Central de Arquitectos (SCA).[20] Although the architects did not insist on making the entire site a park (as did the Asociación Amigos de la Ciudad and the newspaper *La Nación*), they centered their critique on the expected cost of the project, the absence of a global plan that would act as framework for the intervention, and the involvement of the Catalan urban planners. They wanted to replace them with a group of local experts that emerged from a competition sponsored by the SCA.

For us it made no sense to reproduce the formal inflexibility of past master plans, which did not identify venues of action apart from the urban code and public works. More recent experiences (such as the Spanish case) proposed the development of strategic guidelines for choosing among things that could or should be done, and especially for those that had the potential to generate a chain reaction. Overcoming inertia was the main goal of these operations.

Recognizing urban space as the material support of a social structure, we were aware that any intervention in this space would affect diverse social forces. A plan, as expressed by Carlos Matus, was therefore a precise calculation of how to produce a deliberate alteration in a system of forces, with results oriented toward con-sciously chosen objectives.[21] Within this framework, the role of the project was that of an unbalancing element, capable of generating the energy necessary to liberate decision-making on the scale required for such a large enterprise. The relationship between the intentions of a plan and its materialization necessarily leads to an analysis of power.

As we moved toward implementation of the project, power was an issue at several junctures.[22] The decree that established the Corporation indicated that it would receive no state resources apart from land. That the project would not draw on scarce public resources was one of its main strengths. Economic restrictions governing the first development stage increased the power of the business groups, which threatened to seize control of the project.

The use of information was also an expression of power. Media-based discussion of the feasibility of this enterprise put us at the mercy of powerful lobbies, but as we developed the project (and expanded relationships with others who had successfully led similar interventions), we strengthened our leadership.[23]

The city council[24] followed the project carefully and waited for us to ask for their intervention.[25] They aspired to facilitate the project at each step of its materialization. We preferred, however, to rely on existing urban codes rather than seek special rulings.[26] This was a tactical move: formally present the master plan based on existing codes and therefore not invite modifications.[27]

Finally, the mayor and the president of the SCA signed an agreement[28] that required the municipal administration to sponsor a competition to define the master plan. This agreement enabled the commercialization of the old buildings—the first stage. The agreement eased the debate, and—with the support of the architectural association—lessened the councilors' critiques.

The main concession was to give up the project that had been developed with the Spanish team. Faced with the prospect of a competition, I had some fears: that the designers might propose objects on a grand scale without understanding the complexity of the operation; that in the requirements, an old-fashioned attitude about program and zoning could prevail; that financial planning might not be adequately considered and the economic fragility of cash flow properly understood; and—above all—that the time taken in preparation might exceed the political moment I had to deliver concrete results.

The Viability of the Operation

At first, we expected the urbanization of 170 hectares. Of these, 39 hectares were water, 14 were taken up by the highway that crosses the downtown, connecting the north and south of the city, 8 were reserved for access streets, and 17 were taken up by sixteen old dock buildings. In all, 92 hectares remained as land for new urbanization. Of these, 34.5 were to become streets and sidewalks, 13 were for green space, 6 had buildings to be renovated, and 38.5 hectares were left for commercialization.

When calculating the buildable area, the first master plan established ratios that, according to the existing building code, allowed a total of 2,842,100 square meters of construction. As a result of the negotiation with the SCA, green areas were increased, and buildable areas reduced by half. These new numbers reduced the expected land value, thereby increasing the financial risk of the operation. These numbers included the general cost of infrastructure that, if the bridges were modified, would increase; the cost of green areas (including the renovation of Costanera Sur); and a projection of administrative costs (commercialization, administration, security, maintenance, etc.). It was estimated that by the end of the operation, there would be a sizeable surplus to be transferred in equal parts to the national and municipal administration.

The First Sales

The invitation for bids for a first package of five warehouses spurred interest. The presence of an international investor[29] strengthened local expectations. According to our estimating criteria, the docks—in the state they were in—could each be valued at around U.S. $600,000. In relation to their potential (building area around 10,000 square meters), that value could be increased to $1,500,000.[30] At a time when all payments were made in cash, the Corporation linked payments with the finishing of planned infrastructure. The operative rules were to not sell all the buildings in a block and to prevent interested parties from buying more than two buildings.

We feared the possibly uneven architectural quality of the proposals, the mix of resulting uses, and the possibility that speculative maneuvering could delay the materialization of the project. To address these concerns, a two-part bidding mechanism was established.[31] The business community responded strongly to the warehouse offerings, and bids surpassed our estimates.[32]

The general project of infrastructure was contracted to the consulting firm Latinoconsult, which oversaw the urban engineering. The work was bid by sections, accompanying the process of land sales. The flow of payments from different buyers allowed the work to advance consistently, with adequate cash flow.[33]

Soon after a new administration took office, Mayor Fernando de la Rúa decided to appropriate the success of the project and declared Puerto Madero a new neighborhood within the city. To strengthen his candidacy as president of Argentina, he sped up the sale of sites. The need to complete the construction of infrastructure produced a loosening of the bidding requirements, such as the need to present architectural projects and make commitments to a given pace of construction. This lowered the quality of the enterprise. The project continues to be developed, but not without threats to its full realization. The role of the Corporation, going forward, is still unclear. Is it the most apt mechanism to preserve and transfer the experience acquired in the development of Puerto Madero? Might it be useful as an instrument to take charge of other state lands that—as in the case of some railyards—may have a strategic importance for urban development or the enhancement of other parts of the country?

Conclusion

What would be success, and what would be failure? What should be the parameters for evaluating this experience? A first valuation criterion is related to the capacity of Puerto Madero to meet its own objectives.

Alfredo M. Garay

The results are visible. The central area of the city recovered vitality, as the effects of the intervention extended beyond the specific area of the project. Toward the north, in the Catalinas area, the built area for offices doubled. Toward the west, the band between the Madero and Paseo Colón avenues has experienced considerable development. Although in the southern area of Puerto Madero only the first residential buildings are being opened, the urbanization is planned to expand over other industrial sites in the area.

The opening of plazas, parks, and other public spaces brings together large groups of people, particularly residents of the southern area of the city who populate these new places. What was built clashes in some ways with the "elite" early outline of the project. Building owners have to accept the impossibility of enforcing class exclusivity, given that 40,000 people cross the place each weekday. Everything seems to confirm the view that in Puerto Madero, the climate of the downtown will be reproduced, so I do not fear that the area will be consolidated as an exclusive enclave.

The project's contributions to economic development are impressive: all of the sites have been sold for more than U.S. $240 million. Of 2 million expected square meters of development, 800,000 have been built, generating more than 20,000 jobs. The Corporation has paid U.S. $27 million to the state in taxes.

From an urban point of view, still to be considered are the effects of the transfer of central activities and the eventual appearance of rundown areas downtown, where old office buildings are concentrated. This type of intervention must be a part of a group of policies that aim to revitalize the downtown—for example, promoting the recovery of this area as a residential zone. The abandonment of other urban policies dilutes the expected results and jeopardizes the success of the overall operation.[34] The paradox is that critique tends to center on the action, and rarely are the effects (and costs) of inaction taken into account.

The development of Puerto Madero leaves us with some lessons:

- It confirms the possibility of large-scale interventions. It allows us to understand the complexity of interactions among social actors.
- It requires translating ideas from an urban-architectural rationale to one of politicians and others who deal in power relationships.
- It underlines the usefulness of implementing new administration mechanisms.
- It focuses our attention on the hold of inertia and the culture of resistance to change; but at the same time it teaches us that the positions of different parties can change as the transformations of reality facilitate new points of view.

Above all, it demonstrates that it is possible to promote an expansion of economic activity, maintaining a measure of independence from powerful business interests and incorporating political objectives without compromising the integrity of the intervention.

After working for more than ten years on this project, I am particularly interested in the possible transfer of lessons to other contexts and scales. A local government confronting the urbanization of vacant land, for example, might calculate how to combine a park with some income-generating activity.[35] Director General Pablo Otaola has related how, when they began the project of the Ría de Bilbao, they considered the case of Puerto Madero, believing that if in Buenos Aires an intervention of such magnitude was possible, the operation they were considering would be feasible. It gives me hope to believe that this essay will be read by students from many countries, some from poor countries such as mine. I hope it encourages them to try to realize their dreams with the resources they have available.

Notes

1. People from Buenos Aires are called *porteños*—inhabitants of the port.

2. The program was established within the framework of the celebration of the 500th anniversary of the discovery of America, with financing from Spain that covered half of the investment. A municipal office was created that served as mediator between owners, businesses, and inhabitants of properties along the dilapidated avenue, promoting its renovation. In three years this program achieved the renovation of twenty-five buildings and forty-five interventions at the ground-floor level.

3. PRAM was in charge of the Consejo de Planificación Urbana and had the support of IPU (Inventario de Planificación Urbana, a nongovernmental organization dedicated to the preservation of patrimony) and PROSUR (an administrative entity that emerged from an agreement with PNUD). It was able to add a new chapter to the urban code Código de Ordenamiento Urbano that identifies areas of historic protection (APH).

4. In the case of La Boca, the first step was the purchase of twenty-one tenements for U.S. $200,000. The Junta De Andalucía supported the work on the block called "manzana De San Francisco." The program RecupBoca was developed with French cooperation.

5. After twelve years of this experience, I realize that Puerto Madero was stronger than the other interventions we had undertaken. The historic preservation statements added to the urban code had limited scope (and did not prompt, as I expected, historic preservation in other downtown areas). The program Avenida de Mayo was abandoned when our administration left office, and in relation to the renovation of tenements, subsequent mayors were so opposed to the policy that they did not even participate in the opening ceremonies. The policies for the central area, however, were only part of the tasks assigned to the planning office. For example, planning and administration workshops included neighborhood organizations in surveying needs and formulating proposals—resulting in projects that, during the three years of our administration, were 70 percent completed.

6. By the mid-1980s the Administración General de Puertos had commissioned Rogge Marin to undertake a study of the ports; this report considered the abandonment of port uses in a large area of Puerto Madero and recommended its urbanization.

7. This document had three parts: a brief outline of concepts, an evaluation of financial feasibility, and images that documented proposed changes.

8. The transfer of land for the materialization of the operation required approval by the National Congress, but in the context of a deep economic crisis, two laws that simplified the transfer mechanism were passed, allowing the president to decide which properties were unnecessary to the administration.

9. Even in the first three years, the management structure consisted of not more than thirty people.

10. For the competition "20 Ideas para la Ciudad," we provided, in the form of a manifesto, a listing of criteria for the implementation of urban policy.

11. It was also the moment when Ted Raymond, who had developed the Navy Yard in his native Boston, approached the newly established Corporation and with great generosity provided us with invaluable experience.

12. The Spanish advisors included Jordi Borja, Joan Busquets, and Joan Alemagni.

13. The municipal team included Jorge Moscato, Emilio Rivoira, Nestor Magariños, and Pablo Huberman, with the support of Carlos Rodríguez, Silvia Fajere, and Mishal Katz.

14. As a result of the negotiation, business interests had the municipality as an ally in the transformation of port operations; the city lobbied Congress to transfer port operations from national to local governments (provincial or municipal).

15. This was not a cohesive group so much as a collection of independent actors.

16. I must confess that given the potentially risky creation of the Corporation during a time of economic crisis, the arrival of internationally prominent investors with an interest in our project increased our optimism.

17. He met not with the board of directors of the Corporation or the mayor, but with the president. The president lacked sufficient information to formalize an agreement, but suggested that Trump meet with us for in-depth discussion.

18. That consisted in financing the construction of infrastructure and public space, funding the operation of the Corporation, and transferring earnings (calculated at the time at U.S. $150 million) to the municipality and the national administration, in equal shares.

19. Until then, there been no enterprise with an investment of over U.S. $30 million. Office towers that were frequently built (two per year, according to market research) required an investment of around U.S. $10 million, and the bulk of construction (apartment buildings within the urban fabric) was the result of investments of U.S. $3–$5 million.

20. In the most important meeting organized by the SCA, participants urged priority for leisure and recreation functions, and questioned the need for continued concentration of other activities downtown. They wanted a plan for the entire metropolitan area.

21. Carlos Matus, *Estrategia y Plan* (Mexico: Siglo XXI Editores, 1981).

22. As I have done elsewhere, I cite the analysis by Angel Panebianco in Modelos de Partido to support my arguments.

23. The Catalan group emphasized the need to systematically study other contemporary enterprises. They gave us the tools to critically rethink the Catalan case and to incorporate lessons from other interventions such as those of Baltimore, Battery Park, Boston, and the Docklands, as well as the APUR (Atelier Parisien d'Urbanisme) experiences.

24. At the time, the city council was called Consejo Deliberante and had sixty members, with only thirteen from the ruling party. Later the new city constitution changed the name and characteristics of this legislative body.

25. The planning office (Secretaría de Planeamiento) was in conflict with the Consejo Deliberante. The Código de Planeamiento Urbano sanctioned by the military government in 1976 was a restrictive code that was full of inconsistencies; the legislative body would authorize through exceptions things that were not allowed. This process led to some abuses, so soon after taking office we proposed a new procedure for making modifications to the code.

26. During the military government a megaproject had been proposed, called Ensanche Area Central (EAC), which promoted the creation of a large landfill at the river's edge. The government designated

Alfredo M. Garay

the area for "special urbanization" and assigned parameters that, for our project, were quite convenient.

27. When there is an acquired right, no other norm may be applied retroactively.

28. Four points were key to the development of the enterprise:

    1. The Corporation and the municipal administration would sponsor an ideas competition, with the SCA.

    2. The competition referred exclusively to the east sector, given that the west (the line of sixteen docks) was to be commercialized by the Corporation. The Corporation could begin preliminary development, according to a preservation strategy to be agreed upon with the legislature.

    3. The competition requirements be the basic program and criteria of the master plan developed with the Catalan consultants.

    4. There would not be one winner, but three. The Corporation would hire three members of each winning team to develop, with experts from the Corporation, the final master plan.

29. Ted Raymond.

30. The cost was U.S. $150 / square meter.

31. A first envelope contained the architectural project, program, and a phased investment plan. It also had to include a feasibility study, previous projects sponsored by investors, and a bank warranty. With these elements, the Corporation could evaluate which proposals offered quality, credibility, and convenience in relation to the general objectives of the project. Only those who passed the first evaluation were allowed to submit a second envelope, in which they presented their bid for the property.

32. The value offered for the first dock was around $6 million (four times the expected amount). This figure fell to $3 million on average for the rest of the sales. The numbers presented by one investor considered a cost of construction of about U.S. $10 million, with an expectation of a selling price after construction of $2,000 / square meter.

33. The Corporation has sold land for a total value of $240 million. Still remaining for commercialization are the lots of dock 4, which are destined for towers. They were not able to be commercialized because they are occupied by the playing fields of the Colegio Nacional de Buenos Aires; the Corporation has been put in charge of their relocation, which will provide new and better sports facilities.

34. The policy of revamping Avenida de Mayo was abandoned in 1993, and in 1995 the authorities of the new city administration announced that they would dedicate themselves to the rehabilitation of Corrientes avenue. Without a clear strategy or an administrative model, the work was limited to a change in sidewalk materials. Since 1993 there has been no talk of policies for social housing, nor are there any initiatives to restore the residential character of the downtown. The norm sanctioned in 1992 has not been accompanied by the work of identification and classification of areas needing historical protection. Limited to applying the existing norm, and not expanding the limits of protected areas, the city administration cannot stop the demolition of buildings of value or promote private interventions in the existing fabric.

35. For example, the new urban center of Malvinas Argentinas in the urban periphery of Buenos Aires.

Dock 4, leisure facilities

The Architecture of Puerto Madero in the 1990s

Claudia Shmidt

The architecture for the new Puerto Madero emerged full of mandates, premises, assumptions, and objections. The development of the program was the product of an important debate channeled through government, corporate, and private interests, with a high point in the 1991 national competition, Concurso Nacional de Ideas. The instructions to repair the "mistakes" of the past and recover "values" that should not have been lost were based on displeasure with the contiguous Catalinas—its "lack of character," the limitations of strict zoning, the generation of dead zones, an excessively tight fabric that resulted in a visual barrier created by the repetition of towers, the inhospitable ground level.

This critical view opposes what were in the 1960s and 1970s modern impulses given form when Catalinas was becoming the symbol of economic development, as the great headquarters of multinational corporations that would find in Buenos Aires a place to expand the network of economic relations. Its grid was rotated 45 degrees, in opposition to the overwhelming orthogonal grid that structures the city. Its aim was to resemble the towers that define "city" in New York or Frankfurt, isolating the few points of resistance such as the Conurban building.[1]

Many of the architects who built Catalinas are the same ones who would develop the Puerto Madero program and request for proposals, and obtain the awards and develop the master plan for the port revitalization. This overlap, however, does not imply a contradiction. Picking up fragments of post-CIAM debates, or heeding the lessons of local experience, they were in search of an argument for a new urbanization. They had to act, because the area had owners but not inhabitants—lands, buildings, water, infrastructure, trash, landscapes, but almost no people. Only the postcards of a bygone era when everything was frenzied activity.

The development's program aimed to determine the social profile of the occupants: offices, apartments, recreation amenities, hotels, higher education facilities, sophisticated spaces for an artistic presence. Keeping in mind that the project is about the transformation of public lands (the most expensive in Buenos Aires and

Panoramic view

The program is somewhat similar to the one represented by the Impressionists during the years of the transformations of Paris by Haussman. As noted by Thomas Crow, Meyer Schapiro would warn of the complicity between modernism and consumer society that could be clearly read in Impressionist paintings, which would create images of its new material culture as urban idylls, from the point of view of a relaxed spectator.[2]

The reference to the second half of the nineteenth century is not accidental. The effort to provide a particular character, in the manner proposed by Quatremère de Quincy (to create architecture that can say with certainty what it is and discard what it is not), strongly underlies the master plan. To regulate uses, define programs, establish typologies, preserve / modify cultural value, to maintain homogeneity—these are some of the possible ways to achieve a balance between those urban idylls and the reality of a neighborhood in the heart of the metropolis.

Another premise of the program was to reinforce the idea of being "porteño" for its symbolic value. To be "porteño," literally speaking, is to be from the port. But in Argentina, the *porteño* is the inhabitant of Buenos Aires—above all, as federal district—in clear opposition to the people from the interior provinces. It is about a masculine character constructed by tango mythology (the *guapo*, the *piola*), whose typical habitat is the area of Corrientes street, near the Obelisco. In any of its forms, the storied "porteño" has actually little to do with the port, even less with the river. It is possible that the quality of being "porteño" is the weakest argument in the construction of the discourse.[3]

But if the quality of being "porteño" remains rhetorical, the revaluation of preexisting qualities will in fact play a decisive role. The maintenance of the grid will be the surest of bets for promoting the integration of Puerto Madero with Buenos Aires. Perhaps because it is the urban experience of longest duration, the "block" together with the warehouses will remain untouched.

among the most expensive in the country), public spaces and parks were proposed. The program includes various typologies, backed by strong building codes: free perimeter buildings, towers, perimeter organizations around courts.

The Corporación Antiguo Puerto Madero is a state corporation but without a state budget; it is administered as a private company, its capital derived from the sale of lands at a high price per square meter, based on their prime location within the city. However, what would it mean—in strictly architectural terms—to administer the state capital as a private company? It seems that in the case of Puerto Madero, the architecture must respond to a predetermined market demand, starting with the assumption that the target buyer / inhabitant / user will belong to a Class A consumption group (large multinational companies, members of the bohemian bourgeoisie, five-star tourists).

Panoramic view

View of Puerto Madero East

Claudia Shmidt

The arrangement is primarily organized, asymmetrically, by a north-south axis formed by the four docks. The west side maintains the skyline of the city, with the strength provided by its extension along the length of the old warehouses, with an English engineering language of the nineteenth century. On the opposite side is the island that relegates public parks to a third plane. Transversal connections are maintained through the extension of avenues that reach the island with rotating bridges. But the visual communication is complex. From the city there are few continuous vistas, because the location of warehouses corresponds to the division in equal intervals of the limits of each dock and acts as closure of the perspectives of the crossing streets.

From the precinct of the docks, on the other hand, this subtle "lack of order" is adopted for the organization of the grids of the project, although strictly in an east-west direction. The relationship with the Río de la Plata is difficult. Strictly speaking, the Puerto Madero urbanization is centered in its own "interior" river. The stepped section, from the lowest blocks along the east shore of the dock to the top of the perpendicular axis with the towers (probably isolated and out of proportion with the final skyline), generates ascending perspectives that tend to stand out because of the generous sky views allowed by the massing.

The insistence on maintaining the block, understood as a perimeter organization around an open central space, was so strong that the proposals that made this premise relative were overlooked. The variant of

narrow lots—without the possibility of an interior patio—aligned along the east shore of the docks results in an excessively elongated massing that produces an adequately scaled base, although it generates forced solutions given its extreme length. The layout will result in an atypical fabric that offers a sui generis partition: the blocks of traditional layout, rectangular in shape, push to the limits the conditions of the needed open center, and the narrower lots produce pieces made up of repetitive modules; the idea of a service street between them does not exist as in the layout of New York. Everything is then transformed into a succession of *grandes façades* articulated in three different stepped heights. This ensemble, especially at the east side, achieves a totally new urban landscape for Buenos Aires. The complete absence of the "medianeras"—the emblematic irregular and massive lateral walls of the city buildings—creates an amazing effect. The sequence of clean horizontal toplines and the continuity of the

façades, framed at an unexpected human scale, offer an interesting and still unexplored urban experience.

One of the key strategies for the excellence of the final architectural project resides in the manner in which these strong conditions are taken into account. At the request of CAMPSA, the office Estudio Aisenson developed the project Madero Plaza in a rectangular block with an open core, at dock 2. From a preliminary study of alternatives emerged the possibility of locating apartments and offices with a retail ground floor for that type of lot, without an open structure of pilotis, but actually enclosed. The proposal intended to break up the perimeter massing required by code and transform the "fact" of the interior patio into a plaza of public access that would at the same time organize the entries into the units. With a refined solution designed to avoid the mansards suggested by code, the office made a key technical decision: by locating water tanks and elevator machine rooms and other services in the basement

Claudia Shmidt

levels, it obtained an independence of volumes, a flat and decisive top, and optimal ventilation in the interior plaza. The transparency and permeability of this alternative follows a line of thought pursued by the Aisenson office in various projects throughout the country, but it also challenges the familiar conceit of the block that retains a forbidden space in its interior.[4]

The master plan envisioned the sale of smaller lots of 16 or 30 meters wide by 14 meters deep. Although the sale resulted in the acquisition of whole or half blocks, the old scheme was maintained and therefore generated unequal solutions. One land occupation alternative was put forward by César Pelli and Associates, who proposed opening the "U" toward the east dock. But in other cases, such as that of Dujovne-Hirsch, located on the site of the demolished Bunge y Borne silos, a convex façade creates a "U"-shaped interior space; the orientation and height of this approach condemns a good part of the interior front to extended periods of shade.

The harshness with which the master plan requires the resolution by typologies limits the possibility of the development of types. In this sense Argan's explanation (following Quatremère) about the difference between the concept of *type* (implying the idea of a "vague" or undefined object) and that of *typology* (presupposing a value judgment based on a resolution strategy) seems to apply.[5] However, does it make sense to continue to claim these relationships for a contemporary metropolitan development? In other words, is the relationship between project and use still in effect in the search for quality or character for Puerto Madero? If so, how can a destination point be thought of? To follow this line of inquiry can lead to several paths. One of them is Vittorio Magnago Lampugnani's question: "What remains of the modern project?"[6] The Italian critic presents the sustainability of architecture as opposed to current worldwide economic mechanisms. Finding value in location, and not architecture, is a result of building speculation

of advanced capitalism, but in no way of the modern project. In contrast, Michael Speaks presents the dilemma of "remaining" within what he calls the "moralizing theater of modernism," or alternatively to accept as "positive and opportunistic" that which the market reveals, understood as a "new condition of possibility."[7]

Could it be said that the architecture of Puerto Madero follows market leads as Speaks says, displacing the search for the new in order to pay attention to what "is there"? If we accept this reading, Puerto Madero would not be much different from Kop van Zuid in Rotterdam or Canary Wharf in London, for example. This, however, it is about an endeavor in a large city located, according to global jargon, in an "emerging" country. What possibilities exist for such a country, especially one that has lost economic credibility?

Paradoxically, the Puerto Madero development seems to base its trust in the construction of an urban scenario built in relation to the figure of a relaxed spectator. It creates the illusion of homogeneity organized around compositional elements that, at first sight, surprise because of their ingenuity: compact massing, regular façades with mansard setbacks, streets or boulevards

that articulate heights and the relationships between blocks. But it is not about a search for equal opportunities, for standards or uniformity, in the sense of the modernist premises of the first decades of the twentieth century; rather it is about a pragmatic operation of style, about the effort to respond to a determined international style.

The unanimous call from owners, developers, and entrepreneurs to assemble local and well-known international architectural offices reveals the conditions of the development. The participation of renowned global companies with headquarters in the United States or Europe and offices in strategic parts of the world is a new phenomenon in Argentina, within the context of an apparently deregulated economy. The influence of the multinational company in these endeavors is vast

and includes the development of the design project and the importation of much of the technology of the building. The role of the local office is in general supervisory, of controlling the materialization of the project. One example is the building for Telecom by Kohn, Pedersen, Fox with architects Hampton, Rivoira, and Associates.[8]

In any event, there was no place for aesthetic testing or speculation. Even fashions—and perhaps this is a good thing—are questioned when they present themselves as ephemeral.[9] On the other hand, known firms were welcomed and "signature" architectures accepted, as brands that are a guarantee of international approval and consumption. But the "signature" architects fit a predetermined profile. They are not avant-garde architects, understood as those adopting attitudes of radical change within the context of architectural culture. Those offices that, because of their particular imprint, generate attention that overshadows the context were not invited either. Who then are the "appropriate" architects for Puerto Madero? Who has to be well treated, the relaxed spectator or an investor who doesn't want risks greater than those required by investments in a country with conditions of economic instability? What is a "safe" architecture? In parallel, the position taken by the city of Rosario—that over the same time period is generating a phenomenal transformation—is considerably different: Alvaro Siza, Oriol Bohigas, and Rem Koolhaas have all been called in for diverse architectural and urban interventions.

Clearly, the level of investment risk is the determining factor for the architecture of Puerto Madero. The most literal case is the project for the ING insurance company, developed by the office of Manteola, Sánchez Gómez, Santos, Solsona, Salaberry. Conceived with almost historicist aesthetic principles, the volume over a half-block site responds to the requirement of the client: to represent the image of "strength and soundness." The team of architects used a red granite surface covering a perforated wall. On the back, a volume in aluminum and glass emerges. Tradition, solidity, currency—ingredients of a sure formula. Certainly quite different from the one the same office boldly used during the 1980s when building the new image of the Banco de la Ciudad de Buenos Aires with a materiality opposed to tradition: glass boxes and transparency, signaling availability.

In Puerto Madero, the official language—if the term is allowed—is expressed in a tendency toward the neutral, as a strategy to eliminate unwanted tension or vanguardisms. The accent on horizontal lines, the use of technology (although in many cases the doubtful quality of the glass puts at risk the desired effect), and the predictable volumes are some of the most generalized elements used in what has been produced to this day. We could say that it is about a modernism without anxiety, which contrasts with the "anxious modernism"[10] of the 1960s that characterized the

towers of Catalinas. It is not by chance that the towers built in the 1990s in the same area show off their tops as a sign of individual identity, a tendency that follows international trends.

Within this general scene, some pieces stand out for their quality. One is the Museo Fortabat by Rafael Viñoly Architects PC. One should view this work in relation to another contemporary phenomenon: the construction of art museums, by private initiatives, in Buenos Aires. Within the economic context of the 1990s, the battle to become the cultural capital of the Mercosur was fought between São Paulo and Buenos Aires. The Argentine capital thus sees buildings being designed specifically for museums for the first time in its history.[11]

Amalia Lacroze de Fortabat, the owner of the largest cement company in the country, went directly to Rafael Viñoly, with the confidence of obtaining a high-quality product whose originality would produce a timeless image.[12] The siting, on one of the best lots of Puerto Madero, strongly restricted the designer because of its dimensions and required occupation permits. Yet while the patron shares with the community her art collection and donates a cultural space, Viñoly offers an appealing novel vision of Buenos Aires. The opaque and solid base supports a glazed 135-degree vault that, when turning two-thirds of its circular section toward the east front, generates vistas back toward the city, precisely toward Catalinas. The novelty is to allow the building, from a high point, to turn itself toward the urban profile of Buenos Aires, as if seen from the river. This is one of the most interesting offerings of the whole east dock of Puerto Madero—the visual spectacle made available to the public through the museum. A neat system of light-regulating devices will produce the effect that in the interior of the museum, art and spectators are sheltered. Sensitive to changes in light and heat, by both day and night, Viñoly's cupola suggests an emotional experience that produces silence, the unproductive dilemma between the building as a work of art and the value of the collection to be exhibited: collectively they provide a multiplicity of overwhelming sensations.

As a gift to the city, the owners of the Hilton (the Grupo González) commissioned a pedestrian bridge from Santiago Calatrava. Located behind the historical axis,

Views of Puerto Madero West

the Catalonian's piece offers great style. The work—one part in concrete, prefabricated in situ, and an exuberant steel piece imported from Spain—was baptized "Bridge of the Woman," and is said to be inspired by the tango. For the normal use of the setting there was no real need to add a crossing, thus the piece presents itself as the fourth bridge and is eminently sculptural. However, it ends somewhat forced in the west margin, on the side of dock 3, and therefore makes the perspective view weaker.

Maybe for such a reason the possible future postcard views of the bridge will be the frontal views—from the north or south—and some careful lateral views. The most difficult shot will be the one taken from the west, not only because of its position relative to the general composition, but because it will inevitably contrast with the mythical photograph of Horacio Cóppola.[13] The Borgean climate of such an image was made possible by the superposition of horizontal planes, comprised of traditional elements and pure modern forms.

In terms of the preservation of elements that have material, cultural, or historic value, the decision to maintain the forceful line of storage depots has been a step in the right direction. Yet extremists would have preferred that, in addition to preserving the brick façades, there had been a requirement to keep intact the interior steel and wood structures. For the relaxed spectator, for the bourgeois bohemian, an industrial profile is not adequate unless it is mediated by veils of nostalgia or the evidence of time passed. For this, the context would be that of the urban idyll.

Quite curious is the adoption of the English term "dock" for the warehouses. Perhaps the word mistakenly applied to the brick buildings was taken from the original plans by Parsons and Bateman. The code allowed minor changes to them, such as additions to top levels or changes in the short-side façades. For the recycling of these units, the various offices that participated used formulas respectful of the main massing and varied in the artifacts added to the brick mass. Of particular interest are the installations of the Universidad Católica[14] that occupy three of the sixteen warehouses of Puerto Madero. Each piece was treated independently, trusting the unit to the homogeneity produced by the main-

Claudia Shmidt

Madero Plaza building, plan and elevation (Estudio Aisenson)

tenance of the original brick façades of the east and west fronts, reinforced by the gallery as public space that distinguishes the university complex from other uses.

The only volume that was part of the extensive succession of brick buildings that had to be totally rebuilt is dock 8, whose original structure was badly damaged. The project was assigned to a group of local architecture offices—Baudizzone, Lestard, Varas, and Mariano Billick, Associates with Carlos Díaz and Oscar Fuentes—and it constitutes a unique piece that reinforces the strength of the warehouses. Transparent volumes toward the docks and opaque ones toward the city comprise a balanced play in black and white, with the added value of producing high-quality interior space.

Meanwhile, in the area of the island, discreteness seems to have prevailed over theoretical, historical, or even economic criteria. It is difficult to identify the preservation policy and criteria for making exceptions; witness the arbitrariness of the preservation of the

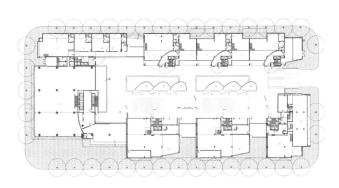

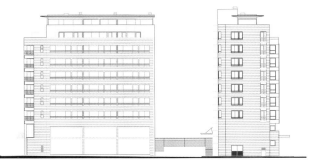

characteristic silos of the port and in the parks. In this sense, the conceptual separation between "public spaces," "new green areas," and "Costanera Sur revitalization" highlights a problem that arises from poorly defined variables.

In a first stage, the construction of the pedestrian walkway between the warehouses and the docks was commissioned from the office of Hampton, Rivoira, and Associates, understanding this area as an independent unit. The gray and constrained intervention relies on the strength of the paving stone, a granite cobblestone that once characterized the paving of the whole city but that since the 1970s, with the arrival of asphalt, has become an element of nostalgia. The handrail, constructed from basic metal pieces, together with the thinness of the lighting columns, provide an understated context for the sophisticated, beautiful, and bold pieces

of urban furniture designed by Diana Cabezas. The "seats for the city" (as defined by their designer) are directly related to the tradition of urban furniture in the metropolitan parks of Buenos Aires and stand out for the exquisite reworking of those organic-academic forms that are already a part of the urban memory, and for careful application of durable materials: wood, steel, concrete, granite.

In a second stage, a competition was called for the "new green areas and revalorization of Costanera Sur." The use of a conservation strategy for the Costanera Sur was based on the search for a nostalgic effect. But, in opposition to other similar actions—the conservation of the warehouse façades or the positioning of cranes as typical objects—the strength of the original work and the contemporaneity of its elements come into conflict with the necessary temporal or spatial dis-

Madero Plaza building, interior views

Claudia Shmidt

tance required by an operation of resignification with a romantic profile.

This piece, of metropolitan scale and excellent architectural manufacture, will connect directly with the new public parks. But that same condition will allow the gathering of a public with a heterogeneous profile, different from the elite public to whom the program of the private sector is directed. This skillful blending will depend on the character of the urbanization. The differences are established. Many aspects of the program offered by the public parks are already provided for the private buyer / inhabitant / user. The housing, hotels, and offices have, for exclusive use and at different scales, areas for leisure, gymnasiums, swimming pools, interior patios, enclosed green areas, and restaurants.

The new public parks envisioned for Puerto Madero maintain somewhat the spirit of American urban parks of the nineteenth century, understood as machines of civilization. Along similar lines, asymmetric but integrated, as currently witnessed between the sophisticated edge of Avenida Libertador and its relationship with the Palermo Park, the proposals selected for the Puerto Madero competition find themselves in the same zone

as its architecture: re-creation of romantic scenes, play and sports areas, tame sculpture parks and art objects, all "under control," without surprises. But the emer-

View of the **ING** building

Museo Fortobat, three views

Views of skyscrapers,
Madero East

realizing that it has been mortally wounded with the elimination of its main condition, contact with the river / ocean. When destroying its reason for existing with the urban dump creating artificial territory—a false shore— it will transform itself into a site without the inner life that gave it meaning. The conservation criteria go against the interest of accentuating nostalgia; they will only generate anguish. It is notable that the two areas of least architectural definition coincide with the sites allocated to these new areas. One of them is the edge that relates the Costanera Sur with the controversial and inaccurately labeled "Ecological Reserve"; the other is the southern area of Puerto Madero currently outlined by the highway.

In the first case, there is a logical attitude, if the high level of indecision and potential conflict surrounding the destiny of the island is considered. In the other case, what surprises is the lack of connection of the metropolitan node of dock 1 and the Dársena Sur or southern dock, accentuated by the solitary Malecón building. This

gence of a new civic consumer will find an obstacle in the brutal relationship between the disproportionate height and density of the residential towers and their impact on the ground level, without major mediations.

But the biggest omission may be the euphemism of the intention to "revitalize" the Costanera Sur without

Claudia Shmidt

piece, designed by HOK and developed by the office Estudio Aisenson, is impeccable from a technical point of view, but it underscores the dilemma between the real-estate business—which required a low-rise building given expected sales—and architecture. What surprises is the conception of a piece of extreme axial symmetry for a location as complex and strategic as the ending of the internal axis of the docks, but highly conflicting in its connection to the city.

As a counterpart to this situation, the strength of the homogeneity, the scale, and the resolution of what has been built so far—in such a short period of time—will contribute favorably to a successful resolution of the public areas. In effect, the great energy concentrated on maintaining the architectural frequency modulation, on imposing a language, consolidates a perception of unity that will contribute to adjusting relationships with the metropolis. And in this sense we must pay attention: the dissonances come from the south.

What is gradually becoming apparent is an orientation toward "urban architecture" and the study of those proactive pieces as part of the generation of the civic realm.[15] At least in those terms, one can hear the noise coming from the Corporación Buenos Aires Sur S. E. This association, of recent creation, emerged from conditions different from those of Puerto Madero. It is in charge of an extended area, mixed in composition—

industries, housing, services—degraded in some areas with the inclusion of squatter settlements, but at the same time with a potential urban and natural landscape unknown within the city. To follow its mandate, it will be necessary to revalue the land. The strategy, in this case, is almost the opposite of that deployed in Puerto Madero. The definition of the profile of the consumer

Universidad Católica Argentina

Dock 8 buildings, three views

Unrestored warehouse

Public space and urban infrastructure

Claudia Shmidt

Malecón building

The Architecture of Puerto Madero in the 1990s

and the elaboration of the master plan are under development based on design research, a methodology that tends to promote a diversity of proposals.

But where in the 1960s and 1970s a clear relationship existed between tradition and modernity within a context of developmental expansion of the countries of the so-called third world, there now appears a more complex picture, and Puerto Madero is part of this reality. The tensions it faces—from the north with the reconversion of the Retiro-Puerto Nuevo area, but above all with the future integration with La Boca and the southern neighborhoods—will influence the metropolitan character of this unique area.

Recycled industrial buildings and silos, Madero East

Claudia Shmidt

Notes

1. Designed by Ernesto Katzenstein for Estudio Kocourek, 1969. J. F. Liernur "La importancia de ser Ernesto," in *Ernesto Katzenstein, 1932–1995* (Buenos Aires: Fondo Nacional de las Artes, 1999).

2. Meyer Schapiro, "The Nature of Abstract Art," *Marxist Quarterly* (1937), citation from Thomas Crow, "Modernism and Mass Culture in the Visual Arts," in *Modern Art in the Common Culture* (New Haven: Yale University Press, 1996).

3. It is confined to the names of the buildings: Porteño Plaza, Los Colonos, Quinta Fundación, Malecón, Puerto Viamonte.

4. The final version was modified. CAMPSA sold the lot with the project, but the new owners changed the program, eliminating the offices. The massing gained in unity, although the interior plaza was no longer public, making it less permeable.

5. Giulio Carlo Argan, *Progetto e destino* (Milan: 1965).

6. Vittorio Magnago Lampugnani, "Cosa rimane del progetto del moderno?" in *Casabella* 677 (April 2000).

7. Michael Speaks, "Dos historias para la vanguardia," in *Block* 5, Universidad Torcuato Di Tella, Buenos Aires, 2000.

8. Built by Benito Roggio e Hijos in association with IRSA, at the north end of Dock 4.

9. As is the case of the nightclub Divino Buenos Aires by Duhalde, Parin Nobili, located in a key space at the North end of both docks.

10. We use this expression in the sense presented by Sarah Williams Goldhagen and Réjean Legault, eds., in *Anxious Modernisms: Experimentation in Postwar Architecture Culture* (Cambridge: MIT Press, 2001). It would be interesting to study in depth the relationship between the contemporary dispassionate production and the vibrant productivity of the 1950s and 1960s.

11. With the MALBA (Museo de Arte Latinoamericano de Buenos Aires), they are the first buildings in Buenos Aires especially designed for art museums. They are added to the Fundación PROA and the Museo Xul Solar as private endeavors whose buildings were recycled for new use.

12. Silvia Pampinella, "Arquitecturas de autor o arquitecturas de mecenas," in *Block* 5, Universidad Torcuato Di Tella, Buenos Aires, 2000.

13. For a discussion of the relationship between Horacio Cóppola and his photographs of Buenos Aires, first conceived during walks through the city with his longtime friend Jorge Luis Borges, see Adrián Gorelik, "Imágenes para una fundación mitológica. Apuntes sobre las fotografías de Horacio Cóppola," in *Punto de Vista* 53, Buenos Aires, November 1995.

14. The design and construction is by the architects Altuna y Asociados.

15. Peter G. Rowe, *Civic Realism* (Cambridge: MIT Press, 1997).

The Architecture of Puerto Madero in the 1990s

Contributors

Alfredo Garay is an architect and urbanist. He was in charge of the Puerto Madero project for the Municipality of Buenos Aires and is currently chairman of the planning and dwelling department of the Province of Buenos Aires administration.

Adrián Gorelik is an architect who holds a Ph.D. degree in history; his dissertation was on the city of Buenos Aires. He is on the faculty of the History of Ideas program of the University of Quilmes.

Jorge Francisco Liernur is an architect and historian. He is chairman of the architecture department at the Torcuato Di Tella University in Buenos Aires.

Luis Javier Domínguez Roca is a geographer. He holds a master's degree in environmental studies and is a Ph.D. candidate at the University of Buenos Aires, where he is on the faculty of the geography department.

Claudia Shmidt is an architect and holder of a Ph.D. degree in history; her dissertation was on the city of Buenos Aires. She teaches at the University of Buenos Aires and at the Torcuato Di Tella University.

Graciela Silvestri is an architect. She completed her Ph.D. in history with a dissertation on landscape in the pampas. She teaches at the University of La Plata and at the Torcuato Di Tella University.

Index

The CASE Series

CASE is a new series on architecture and urban design published in collaboration with Harvard University's Graduate School of Design (GSD). By linking different spheres of knowledge and expertise, CASE aims to reinstate architecture and urban design as synthetic practices that respond effectively to changes in a rapidly developing global economy.

Individual volumes focus on case studies—buildings as well as urban-scale projects—viewed from the perspectives of architects, planners, developers, economists, engineers, sociologists, historians, and theorists. Collectively the authors provide a comprehensive reading of a given project's design, construction, and impact.

Other cases include:

Downsview Park Toronto
Edited by Julia Czerniak

**Le Corbusier's Venice Hospital
and the Mat Building Revival**
Edited by Hashim Sarkis
with Pablo Allard and Timothy Hyde

Toyo Ito · Sendai Mediatheque
Edited by Ron Witte
with Hiroto Kobayashi

Lafayette Park Detroit
Edited by Charles Waldheim

Lucio Costa: Brasilia's Superquadra
Edited by Farès el-Dahdah

For more information, please contact Prestel Publishing.

Illustration Credits